THEY ALL CAN'T
BE RIGHT

Other books by Steve Russo

TruthQuest

THEY ALL CAN'T
BE RIGHT

DO ALL SPIRITUAL PATHS
LEAD TO GOD?

STEVE RUSSO

GENERAL EDITOR: STEVE KEELS

BROADMAN
&HOLMAN
PUBLISHERS

NASHVILLE, TENNESSEE

Published by Broadman & Holman Publishers,
Nashville, Tennessee

Dewey Decimal Classification: 291
Subject Headings: CHRISTIANITY AND
                    OTHER RELIGIONS \ DISCIPLESHIP

1 2 3 4 5 6 7 8 9 10 08 07 06 05 04

Contents

Dedicated to

Tony, Kati, and Gabi.
Thank you for your encouragement and love.
You make my life complete and my heart smile!

Chapter One

Do All Religions
Really Lead to God?

Amy is sixteen and lives in Central Asia where her dad runs an English program. Even though she's an American citizen, she considers Asia much more her home. Amy would also say that she is a strong Christian. Yet in an e-mail message she writes: "In Islam, people believe in one God, and that Muhammad was his prophet, and that Jesus was another prophet, who didn't fulfill God's will when he was on earth (therefore in Islam Jesus isn't God). Anyway the point is that Christians and Muslims and Jews believe in the same God (capital G), all three beliefs are related to Abraham. I hope I don't come across negatively. I love God soooo much (still working on the whole heart) and even more amazing, he loves me!"

As sincere and nice as Amy sounds, she is definitely confused. I've lost count of how many times I've heard someone say, "All religions are pretty much the same, and they will all lead you to God" or "Christianity is no different from any other religion."

A lot of people today think this way. Society says we have to be politically correct and tolerant. People feel the need to affirm all belief systems and avoid giving claim to any single religion as the true "One." The thinking process goes something like this: all religions are equally true and they all deserve the same validation. Plus, it's not good to "close your mind to vast areas of human experience and knowledge." Based on this kind of thinking, you don't have to make any hard decisions that involve a change of lifestyle. You can believe in everything and nothing—all at the same time—without any responsibility.

In a magazine article I wrote, I said that Wicca and Christianity both couldn't be right. Just that comment alone resulted in a bunch of letters from kids and adults telling me how wrong I was and how I shouldn't judge another religion. A seventeen-year-old girl who called herself "Ms. Farrell" was one of the people who sent an e-mail. Here's part of her comments: "You state that both religions (Wicca and Christianity) can't be true. Is it not possible that one God, who created everything, created multiple religions because He or She knew that not everyone would agree on one set framework, because they gave us choice? Thank you for your time. I did not mean this as an insult to your religion. I respect you and I am very glad that you, unlike many others, have found something to believe in as I have."

Doesn't Being Sincere Count?

Some people think it doesn't matter what you believe as long as you're sincere. Ms. Farrell certainly sounds sincere in her beliefs, but being sincere isn't enough. A lot of people are sincere in what they believe. Centuries ago people sincerely believed that the gods at war caused thunder. We now know that their sincere belief was superstition. At one time people also believed that the sun went around the earth, until Galileo demonstrated that this was not true. Once again a sincere belief was not enough. People can be very sincere in what they believe, but they can be sincerely wrong. Just look at the terrorists who carried out their missions on September 11, 2001. Or take Saddam Hussein for example. No one doubts that he was sincere in what he believed, but he was dreadfully wrong.

Don't forget that sincerity is important in our relationships with others. No one likes a hypocrite. But just being sincere isn't enough. I'm always amazed at how often people say that sincerity is all we need when it comes to religion but not to other aspects of life. Stop and think for a minute. You would never say this about a historical event such as World War II. You might sincerely believe that Hitler won the war, but you'd be wrong. Neither would you apply this kind of thinking to mathematics. No one in their right mind would say that if they sincerely believed hard enough, then one plus one would equal three. Why then do we do this when it comes to religion?

Maybe it's because it can be hard to be absolutely sure when it comes to religion. Or maybe we're more concerned with actions than philosophy. On the other hand, it could be because religion is about ultimate issues like life and death, and few of us really want to look at them very closely. We'd rather live for today and not be too worried about tomorrow. It's simply easier to be sincere, do the best we can to live a good life, and hope that it will all count for something in the end.

Let's look at the issue of sincerity in another way. The things that Jesus taught and those that Buddha taught point in essentially different directions. You might sincerely think that Jesus was only a good man and be a sincere follower of Buddha. But what happens if you are sincerely wrong in the end?

Aren't All Religions Basically the Same?

Advances in technology combined with our increasingly more mobile society have turned our world into a global village. Even in small towns it is not unusual to see Jews, Muslims, Hindus, and Buddhists working together and living next door to one another. Because many of them are citizens who have the same rights as those born in this country, it's easy to think that the various religions they follow are pretty much the same as well, that they're only different ways of understanding the same God.

This view is considered politically correct in our tolerant society. In fact, it is true that most religions do have a lot of moral and ethical convictions in common. A number of significant thinkers throughout history have held to this common-sense view. For instance, Mahatma Gandhi said, "The soul of religion is one, but it is encased in a multitude of forms." Still, no matter how appealing this way of thinking might sound, it won't work.

Just ask the actual worshippers within these different faiths if all religions are basically the same. They will all give you a definite no. For some, the more they become convinced of the rightness of their own religion, the more willing they become to slaughter members of other religions and destroy their churches or mosques. For example, it's written in the Qur'an: "Fight and slay the pagans wherever you find them" (Qur'an, sura 9.5). Unfortunately, this is exactly what we see happening today in the Sudan and Nigeria.

Notice how many religions have absolutely opposing views of what God is really like. For example the idea of Wiccan deities has been compared to a family tree, with the "All," or universal energy, at the top. The Lord and the Lady (god and goddess) are the next in line, symbolizing the perfectly balanced male and female aspects of divinity. Finally, closest to humans on earth, are the gods and goddesses. And just like you might choose a friend based on things that you were drawn to instinctively or emotionally, so you can also choose your favorite traits for a god and goddess.

Buddhism has no god and no type of final existence. The Hindu's god is impersonal but can be approached through countless deities and statues. Allah, the Muslim's god, is personal, with no secondary deities and a total ban of idols or any other way of representing Allah. There's no forgiveness or supernatural help in Buddhism and Hinduism, only cold-blooded karma. Christianity, on the other hand, teaches that God is personal, and He not only completely forgives a person; He also offers supernatural assistance to handle the issues of life.

Even when you look at religions that do believe in a personal God, there's no agreement on how and if He shows Himself to us. According to Islam, Allah does not reveal himself in person to humanity. However, Allah does reveal his will, and the only suitable reaction to that is *islam,* which means "submission" (not "peace," as has been frequently suggested since the events of 9/11). In Christianity, God not only reveals Himself to us; He also reveals His will. He did it in the only "language" that we could fully understand—in a human life—through Jesus. That's what Christmas is all about.

Religions also have different views about what the goal of our lives is here on earth or about life after death. A sensual paradise with wine, women, and music awaits Muslims when they die. A Buddhist's life objective is to make it to nirvana—extinction—the "complete cessation of both desire and personality." It took the Buddha only 547 births to accomplish this. To know God and enjoy Him forever is the goal of all existence for Christians. Without a doubt there's a huge difference in what religions teach.

The most significant difference of all is how and if we can make ourselves acceptable to God. Almost all religions stress that following their teachings will enable a person to be fulfilled or reborn. With many religions this involves a form of karma ("cause and effect," paying off your guilt). But this is miles apart from the grace (forgiveness—without cost—when you don't deserve it) of Christianity. The Bible teaches that none of us is capable of saving ourselves or making ourselves acceptable to God. However, the God of Christianity is personal, and because of His awesome love for humanity, He longs to have a relationship with us, making this possible through the shed blood of Jesus.

Don't All Religions Lead to God?

While it may be politically correct to say that all religions lead to God, it's just not possible. If you start examining different religions, you will see that their essential concepts—God, truth, reality, the basic problem of humanity and the solution—are very different. Sometimes they actually contradict each another. Look at atheism and Christianity. Either God exists or He does not. Since the two beliefs contradict each other, logically they both can't be right. Therefore not all religions can lead to God. Let's look at some other examples of diverse types of religions with very different objectives.

- Occult religions—animism, witchcraft, magic, and some parts of New Age. They're about spirits—usually evil ones—that need to be manipulated; they are not about God or a relationship with Him.

- Bourgeois religions that pacify the religious instincts of the wealthy. Self-improvement cults and religions like Christian Science, Theosophy, and Scientology ask very little from their followers except huge amounts of money. They're all about self and not about God.

- Austere religions that are all about self-renunciation, such as Buddhism, Jainism, and even some strands of Hinduism. The self is abandoned and humiliated in order to diminish its grip and to rid the person of being tied to this world. In Buddhism, for example, after many lives you supposedly will finally reach the elimination of the self, which is absorbed into the impersonal "One" or "Monad." It's not about a relationship with God, especially since most of these religions don't even have a God!

- Imperial religions are about the highest ranking political authority, which demands total allegiance. Examples include the divine kings of ancient Egypt, Caesar of the Roman Empire, and Japan's Shinto emperors along with more modern-day rulers like Stalin and Hitler. Both Stalin and Hitler had their own "divine" edges. When Stalin would speak at huge outdoor rallies, he would have pictures of himself projected against low-lying clouds overhead. Hitler liked to use messianic language to talk about himself, and he predicted a Reich of a thousand years.

- Prophetic religions arise from the forceful challenge of a great leader and tend to spread rapidly across the world within a century of their beginning. One example is Islam, which advanced quickly into the Middle East and North Africa within only a few decades of Muhammad's death. However, even Islam with its high view of God doesn't offer its followers intimacy with God: Allah reveals his message. He never reveals himself. Anyone who claims to have intimacy with Allah commits blasphemy and can be executed for doing so.

- Revelatory religions teach that the believer can personally know God. There have only been two religions in history to teach this—Judaism and Christianity. Both maintain that God has given a reliable and personal disclosure of Himself to humanity. In Christianity, however, Jesus Christ claimed to be the fulfillment of all God's promises to Israel and the final revelation of God to humanity. The Bible calls Him Emmanuel—"God with us." A relationship—intimacy— with God is what Christianity is all about. No other religion can make this claim.

How can all religions lead to God when they have such different beliefs about God and how to attain life after death? We don't need a religion; we need a relationship with the living God. Christianity isn't about people in search of God; rather, it's about God in search of people.

Beyond Tolerance to Truth

I've had many teens contact me at *Life on the Edge Live!* (the live call-in radio show I cohost on Saturday nights) to tell me how intolerant I am to think that "my religion is the only one that's got it all right." Unfortunately, they don't really understand what it means to tolerate something. To tolerate something (a belief, viewpoint, etc.) means that you allow it to exist even though you don't agree with it or like it. If I were truly intolerant, I would try to silence other points of view and eliminate them. Just because I disagree with someone, however, doesn't mean I'm intolerant.

Speaking of being intolerant, I've noticed something as I travel across North America speaking on public junior high and senior high school campuses. Before most assemblies, school administrators remind me that I cannot talk to the student body about God, Jesus, or the Bible. Yet, if my assembly contained references to Islam, Hinduism, Buddhism, any other religion, or even alternative lifestyles, I could openly talk about them. Isn't it interesting that in the midst of an era of tolerance, there is great intolerance toward Christianity and Jesus?

It's really not about tolerance; rather, it's about truth. The truth is, there are two enormous reasons why all religions really don't lead to God: the awesomeness of God and the sinfulness of people. Some people who believe that all religions lead to God use the illustration of a mountain with many roads going to the top. They say it doesn't matter which one you take; any of them will get you to the top. This view is invalid—it doesn't work. An illustration that better describes the real situation is that of people trying to find their way through a maze. Many paths lead to dead ends and fail to get them out of the maze. There is only one way through.[1]

Like it or not, we must admit that all religions are not the same. Christianity alone provides the way out of the "maze." The only path to God is through a personal relationship with Jesus Christ. He is the only one who can bridge the gap between a holy God and sinful people. Honestly compare Jesus to all the other religious leaders in the world. When you do, there will be no doubt in your mind why you should choose to follow Him.

Chapter Two

What Does It Mean to Be a Christian?

Before Hong Kong went back to being the property of China, I had the opportunity to travel there and speak at a variety of events. During an interview on a secular radio program, the host of the show asked me, "What is it like to live in a nation where everyone is a Christian?" I was amazed—he honestly thought that everyone living in America was a Christian.

What is a Christian? If you asked twenty people on your campus that question, you'd probably get twenty different answers! After doing an assembly at a high school campus in Iowa, two girls and a guy approached me, wanting to talk. They proceeded to tell me, "We used to be Christians, but now we are Wiccans."

Unfortunately, many people who say they are Christians don't really know what that means. They don't know what they believe, why they believe it, or how to live the Christian life. Let's look at some common misconceptions of what people think makes a Christian.

- *Living a Good Life.* The truth is, no matter how we live, it will never be good enough to reach God's standard of holiness. Check out Isaiah 64:6: "All of us have become like something unclean, and all our righteous acts are like a polluted garment; all of us wither like a leaf, and our iniquities carry us away like the wind." Romans 3:23 says, "For all have sinned and fall short of the glory of God."
- *Going to Church.* Attending church every Sunday doesn't make you a Christian anymore than going to McDonald's

once a week will turn you into a cheeseburger. In Acts 17:22–23 Paul challenged the religious people of Athens that they were missing something.

- *Giving to Others.* It is important to help others, but it is not enough to bridge the gap between you and a holy God.
- *Believing in God.* Just believing won't make you a Christian. The Bible teaches that even the demons believe (James 2:19).
- *Praying.* A lot of people pray, but that alone doesn't make you a Christian, nor does it mean that God even hears your prayers (Job 35:12–13; Ps. 24:3–4; 1 Pet. 3:12).
- *Reading the Bible.* Because you read and know God's Law, that doesn't make you a Christian. Jesus challenged teachers of the law because their hearts were empty (Matt. 23:25–28).
- *Singing Praise Music.* You may only listen to Christian music and sing praise and worship music every chance you get, but it's not enough. Paul warns us about having a form of godliness but denying God's power (2 Tim. 3:5).
- *Being Baptized.* I was baptized at the age of ten, and it had nothing to do with becoming Christian—it was all about joining a church. The Bible is very clear that baptism alone is not enough to make you a Christian (Mark 16:16; Acts 2:38, 41).

So, if living a good life, going to church, giving to others, believing in God, praying, reading the Bible, singing praise music, or being baptized doesn't make you a Christian, what does?

A Real Christian

Let's take an honest look at what it means to be a real Christian. Deciding to become one is the most important decision you will ever make because it not only affects your eternal destiny; it also affects your quality of life here on earth. It's been said that you can be wrong about a lot of things in life, but you better not be wrong about God.

A Christian Knows the Truth

A Christian is someone who has discovered the truth about God's love, forgiveness, and acceptance. In order to become a Christian, we must recognize that we are guilty of violating God's law when we try to live our lives independent of Him. And no matter how hard we try, we cannot save ourselves from the punishment of sin nor can we earn God's love, forgiveness, and acceptance. However, what we cannot do for ourselves, God has done for us in Christ. God's love, forgiveness, and acceptance are guaranteed and secure because Jesus rose from the dead. We are "justified"—made right with God—not by our own efforts to be good enough, but by God's grace (Rom. 5:1).

The awesome thing is that we don't have to try to buy God's love and acceptance because He already loves and accepts us—unconditionally, not if we do this or are worthy, and so forth. Being made right with God is a gift (Rom. 3:24). God simply loves us as we are—not because of our accomplishments, the right things we do, our humility, or even because of our faith. It's like being found guilty of a crime and receiving a full pardon.

But maybe this is why customizing their own religion and designing their own God seems appealing to so many people today—because deep down they don't feel worthy of God's love, forgiveness, and acceptance. The truth is that no one is worthy.

God's love is not blind; He sees us just the way we are and still loves us. We can try to fool others, but we can't fool God. We all try to be someone because no one wants to be a nobody. In spite of us— our open and secret sins, our unlovableness and unworthiness, what we do to ourselves and other people, and the fact that things are not right inside or with others—God still loves us and forgives us (Rom. 5:8).

This was a very hard concept for my grandfather to understand. He was a godfather in the Mafia and was known as "Big Ernie." I was a student in Bible college when I decided it was time to tell him about God's love and forgiveness. When I told him how much God loved him, he stared at me as he smoked a big cigar and said in his raspy voice, "Son, God could never love me. You don't know all the things I've done." I agreed that I didn't know everything about his past, but I told him that God loved him in spite of what he had done. Less than two weeks later, he put his faith and trust in Jesus. Six weeks after that, my grandfather left this life and graduated to heaven.

God is for those who cannot help themselves. In other words, He is for every one of us. God's love is not some kind of mystical reward. It's a gift—absolutely free with no strings attached. His love makes things right between Himself and us. Yet it's not what we do but what God has done.

God loves us, accepts us, and forgives us—without demanding that we be punished for our sin, that we torment ourselves, or that we try to do something to make up for what we have done. It means that our relationship with God has changed, which ultimately changes us—in the way we think and the way we live.

When we realize that God loves us, we no longer live in fear. God's love frees us from the fear of not being good enough or of constantly trying to run from Him. "There is no fear in love; instead, perfect love drives out fear, because fear involves punishment. So the one who fears has not reached perfection in love" (1 John 4:18). Understanding God's love for us—in spite of our sin—should cause us to want to change the direction of our lives, to stop running from God and start following Him. The Bible calls this *repentance*: "For godly grief produces a repentance not to be regretted and leading to salvation, but worldly grief produces death" (2 Cor. 7:10).

Nowadays we don't use the word *repent* in our daily language; however, when the Bible was written, the word was used often. If someone was heading in the wrong direction, he was told, "Repent—you're going the wrong way." In other words, "Turn around." When we discover the truth about God's love, forgiveness, and acceptance, we need to turn our lives around—away from sin and rebellion and back to God.

As Christians, we need to put ourselves in a position where we can regularly hear about and experience God's love. This starts with our own personal study of God's Word and through spending time alone with Him. Hearing about God's love and experiencing it can also occur when attending church and youth group activities and Christ-centered campus clubs. Frequently hearing about God's love will help to build our confidence and our faith.

A Christian Experiences a Changed Life

When we become a Christian, the Bible says that we become a new person: "What this means is that those who become Christians become new persons. They are not the same anymore, for the old life is gone. A new life has begun!" (2 Cor. 5:17 NLT). We're not only reeducated or rehabilitated—we're brand-new creations.

Jesus said that we must be "born again" or "born from above" (John 3:3). In other words, to become a Christian we must be spiritually and supernaturally changed by God's Spirit. This spiritual birth takes place when we decide to turn away from our sins, stop trying to live our lives without God, and begin putting our faith and trust in Jesus. As a Christian, our goal each day should be to become more like Jesus—in our attitude, our behavior, and how we treat others. As we grow in this relationship with Jesus, He will fill more and more of our lives.

Being "born again" also means that we become part of God's family. God adopts us as His children, but He also expects us to live as His children ought to live (John 1:12). Because we are adopted, we have new rights and privileges—as well as a new position with God. This idea is taken from a Roman custom where, in a legal ceremony, the adopted son or daughter was given all the rights of a natural-born child. In this ceremony four things happened:

1. The adopted son lost all rights in his old family.
2. He became heir to his new father's estate.
3. The old life of the adopted person was completely wiped out. For instance, legally all debts were wiped out as if they had never existed.
4. In the eyes of the law the adopted person was literally and absolutely the son of the new father.[1]

A Christian has been restored to a position of favor with God—moved from a place of alienation and hostility to one of acceptance. But keep in mind, not everyone is a child of God. The Bible teaches that He is the Creator of all people, but not the Father of all people. Unfortunately, some people don't want God to be their Father.

Being a Christian means we are set apart by God (sanctified) to leave our sin behind and live a new and radical life. This means that we're not supposed to be conformed to the world and its way of thinking about life. Instead, we should be transformed—changed—in the way we think about life (Rom. 12:2). This happens when the Holy Spirit changes our thinking as we study the Bible, think deeply about how it applies to our daily lives, and do what it says. God doesn't want us to follow the pattern of behavior of those around us at school, in the world, and even at times those at church. Sometimes it's easy to be a poser. You know the routine; let people think you are going along with them—act the part, masquerade—even though inside you disagree. We must radically change the way we think—develop a new attitude about life from the inside—then live it out. Christians refuse to conform to the world because our loyalty to God is more important to us than any other allegiance we may have.

A Christian Follows Jesus and Obeys Him

Being a Christian means that we do not remain "spiritual babies"—still wearing "religious diapers." Just as a child grows physically, a real Christian should be growing spiritually (Eph. 4:14–15). Two key things must happen for us to grow in our faith.

First, we must be fed. "Like newborn infants, desire the unadulterated spiritual milk, so that you may grow by it in [your] salvation" (1 Pet. 2:2). A craving for God's Word marks spiritual growth with the same kind of intensity that a baby craves milk. If we are healthy Christians, we will want to grow. Our spiritual appetites will gradually increase and we will start to grow up. Being a Christian also means we will continually have growing pains; we'll never arrive at some mystical level of spirituality. Growing in Christ is a lifelong commitment.

How strong is your desire to grow spiritually? What kind of spiritual food can you take today: milk or meat? Have you settled for mediocrity, or are you willing to keep on growing—to step out and be a risk taker to see what else God may have for you? Personally, I do not want to get to heaven and hear God say, "Steve, you did OK, but I had all this for you to accomplish, and you wouldn't trust Me. You wouldn't take the risk and step out in faith."

Second, we need to be trained if we want to grow in our relationship with God. "Therefore as you have received Christ Jesus the Lord, walk in Him, rooted and built up in Him and established in the faith, just as you were taught, and overflowing with thankfulness" (Col. 2:6–7). Putting our faith and trust in Jesus is just the beginning of a radical new life. We must also continue to follow Christ's leadership. Every day He wants to guide us and help us with our problems. We need to learn from Jesus—from His life and from His teachings. That means we must take the Bible seriously.

A Christian can only serve one master—Jesus. The Bible describes Him as "Lord of lords and King of kings" (Rev. 17:14). A Christian's life should demonstrate this to be true. When Jesus is Lord, the boss of your life, whatever He says goes! The servant of a king waits for the tiniest hint of a command, then hurries to obey. Likewise, a Christian will do whatever God wants done and go wherever He directs. Jesus has every right to demand this kind of obedience from us because He died for us. When we start to grasp all that Jesus has done for us, it should cause us to want to follow Him.

The awesome thing is that God not only tells us what we need to do; He promises to give us the strength and ability to do whatever He commands: "I am able to do all things through Him who strengthens me" (Phil. 4:13). That's why obeying and serving God is not a burden (Matt. 11:28–30; 2 Cor. 4:7–12). It's a privilege.

We must risk doing what our faith requires—that is, we must live by it. We must stop trusting in ourselves and start obeying God. That includes loving, accepting, and forgiving other people who we don't think deserve it. We need to serve others as Christ would. We must stop ignoring God by trying to live on our own and start trusting Him. Although we will never obey the radical call of Jesus so completely that we will be perfect, the great news is that God still accepts us in spite of our failures.

Jesus was quite clear about the kind of life He requires for those who choose to follow Him. Here are a few examples of things we need to change when we are serious about following Jesus:
- We must give up our fondness for money and material things (Matt. 5:40–42; Mark 10:17–22). We must be willing to give up what belongs to us not because wealth and things are bad but because our confidence must always be in God.
- We must put God before family (Matt. 10:34–39; Luke 9:57–62; 14:25–26). God is not antifamily, but we are not to have any attachment to our family that is so strong that it affects our spiritual growth. Sometimes we can be enslaved by family members and never become all that God wants us to be.
- We must be more than just moral, religious, and pure—we must be holy (Matt. 5:21–48; 6:1–16; Mark 2:15–3:6). Our goal is true and genuine morality and belief—found only in Jesus.

Real Christians are revolutionaries. We should challenge the thinking of those around us—at home, at school, at work, and even at church. The values, ideals, and institutions of the world must be called into question. Our attitude toward the world should be the same as Jesus': we are *against* it so we can be *for* it (John 3:17). In our own power, we can't make the world a better place to live in, but God can—working in and through us.

Is your Christian life challenging and threatening those around you in such a way that they are willing to take Christianity seriously?

Or are you caught up in a "holy huddle" on your campus or in a clique at church? It's time to stop withdrawing. We will only make an impact when we are different from the world *in* the world.

Being a Christian ultimately comes down to a total surrender of your whole self to the living God, whose trustworthiness has been proven by the life, death, and resurrection of Jesus. You become a risk taker because your confidence is in Him. So the question is: are you willing to pay the price it takes to be a follower of Jesus? Do you really want to live a dangerously different, nonconforming life? Many people who first followed Jesus turned away when they heard Him spell out what was required to be a follower of His.

What about You?

Have you decided to put your faith and trust in Jesus yet? Let me help you become a Christian before you read anymore of this book.

You may not completely understand how God places the penalty for your sin on Jesus. Few of us really understand just how much we have been forgiven. But you don't need to understand everything all at once. God only asks you to believe and take the first step.

When you decide to become a Christian, you may not totally understand everything to start with. But as you read the Bible and allow God to teach you, your comprehension will grow.

Keep in mind, this decision will cost you. It will cost you your favorite sins and your self-centered attitude of trying to live your life without God. It may cost you some friends who don't understand why your life is so different. The decision to follow Jesus may even cost you your dreams about the future—God may have something planned for you that you never expected. The cost is high to become a Christian, but it is nowhere near what it will cost you not to become one.

If you're ready to start a relationship with Jesus Christ, take a few minutes right now and follow the "Steps to Peace with God" listed below. It's a simple way to establish an intimate relationship with the living God. Becoming a Christian is the most important decision you will ever make in life. There's nothing greater than experiencing God's love, forgiveness, and acceptance. Once you've made the decision to follow Jesus, life takes on a whole new meaning.

Steps to Peace with God

1. God's Purpose: Peace and Life

God loves you and wants you to experience peace and life—abundant and eternal.

> "We have peace with God through our Lord Jesus
> Christ." (Rom. 5:1)
> "For God loved the world in this way: He gave His
> One and Only Son, so that everyone who believes in
> Him will not perish but have eternal life." (John 3:16)

Why don't most people have this peace and abundant life that God planned for us to have?

2. The Problem: Our Separation

God created us in His own image to have an abundant life. He did not make us as robots to automatically love and obey Him.

God gave us a will and freedom of choice. We chose to disobey God and go our own willful way. We still make this choice today. This results in separation from God.

> "For all have sinned and fall short of the glory of
> God." (Rom. 3:23)
> "For the wages of sin is death, but the gift of God is
> eternal life in Christ Jesus our Lord." (Rom. 6:23)

Our choice results in separation from God. People have tried in many ways to bridge this gap between themselves and God. Our attempts to reach God include good works, religion, philosophy, and morality.

> "There is a way that seems right to a man,
> but its end is the way to death." (Prov. 14:12)
> "But your iniquities have built barriers
> between you and your God,
> and your sins have made Him hide [His] face from you
> so that He does not listen." (Isa. 59:2)

No bridge reaches God—except one.

3. God's Bridge: The Cross

Jesus Christ died on the cross and rose from the grave. He paid the penalty for our sin and bridged the gap between God and people.

"For there is one God
and one mediator between God and man,
a man, Christ Jesus." (1 Tim. 2:5)
"For Christ also suffered for sins once for all,
the righteous for the unrighteous,
that He might bring you to God." (1 Pet. 3:18)
"But God proves His own love for us in that while we
were still sinners Christ died for us!" (Rom. 5:8)
God has provided the only way, and each person must make a
choice.

4. Our Response: Receive Christ

We must trust Jesus Christ as Lord and Savior and receive Him
by personal invitation.

"'Listen! I stand at the door and knock. If anyone
hears My voice and opens the door, I will come in to him
and have dinner with him, and he with Me.'" (Rev. 3:20)
"But to all who did receive Him,
He gave them the right to be children of God,
to those who believe in His name." (John 1:12)
"If you confess with your mouth, 'Jesus is Lord,' and
believe in your heart that God raised Him from the
dead, you will be saved." (Rom. 10:9)

Here's how you can become a Christian:
- Admit your need (I am a sinner).
- Be willing to turn from your sins (repent).
- Believe that Jesus Christ died for you on the cross and rose
  from the grave.
- Through prayer, invite Jesus Christ to come in and control
  your life through the Holy Spirit (receive Him as Lord and
  Savior).

Pray something like this:

Dear Jesus,

*I know that I have sinned and need Your forgiveness. I now
turn from my sins to follow You. I believe that You died on the
cross to take the punishment for my sins and that You came
back to life after three days. I invite You to come into my heart
and life. I want You to be my Savior and Lord. Thank You for
Your love and for the gift of eternal life.*

In Jesus' name. Amen.

Have you decided to establish a relationship with Jesus? If so, you've made the most important decision of your life! This relationship that has started is one that not even death can terminate. It will last forever because Jesus promises to never let you down and never give you up (Heb. 13:5). This is the core of Christianity. It's not a religion: it's God revealing Himself to us, rescuing us from our sin and making it possible for us to have a relationship with Him.

Just as you would in another relationship, remember to stay in touch with your new best Friend. You can do this in a couple of ways. Start by reading the letters Jesus has already given you telling you who He is, how He can help you, how to live your life, and how much He loves you. All this and much more is found in the Bible. Try to take time each day to read and study a portion of it. Also, just as you might "instant message" a friend on the Internet, you can send an instant message to God through prayer. You can pray anytime, anyplace, and you don't even have to be online!

You may feel totally different now, or you may not. The most important thing is that you have started this relationship with the living God. Now you have the rest of eternity to develop it!

And by the way, if you did say a prayer to place your faith and trust in Jesus Christ, please let me know by using the contact information found in the back of this book. This is only the beginning of a great new life with Jesus. I want to pray for you, and I also want to send you some things to help you get started and grow in this new relationship with God.

Think about It

1. Are you a Christian? If not, what are you waiting for?

2. If someone visited your youth group or campus club, would they feel loved and accepted? What can you do to help change things to the way they should be?

3. Is there a part of your life where you are consciously resisting God or disobeying Him? What needs to be done to change this attitude?

Chapter Three

Islam

O ne hip-hop group puts the prophet before the profit, and when they rap, they rap for Allah. Native Deen is a trio of Muslim men who sing only about their faith. They named the group after the Arabic word for "religion" or "way of life." They have two goals: to be role models for music fans who might otherwise be drawn to gangsta rap and they hope to educate Americans about Islam.

"Islam is our daily life," said twenty-nine-year-old Native Deen member Joshua Salaam. "It forms what you do, who you are, what you eat, when you sleep, how you pray, everything. We just sing about what we know and who we are."[1] Native Deen got its start at an annual Islamic youth conference in Minnesota. On the last day, each conference participant would sing or rap on a stage for their peers. Salaam, Abdul-Malik Ahmad, and Naeem Muhammad all met at the conference, struck up a friendship, and the group was formed. Since then, the three have released many singles and cassettes independently over the Internet—enough to gain a following for steady gigs at mosques, weddings, and conferences. The three describe their beliefs as mainstream Islam and won't perform a show where there's mixed dancing or alcohol because both are forbidden under Islam.

Their lyrics address topics such as tensions between Islamic and secular lifestyles, pride in Islamic culture, and fulfilling religious obligations. The chorus of their signature song is "M-U-S-L-I-M, I'm so blessed to be with them." Another tune, "Hellfire," describes the worldly struggles of a halfhearted Muslim who drifts away from his faith and into materialism and drugs before realizing the error of his ways and begging forgiveness from Allah.

The group uses only percussion and voices because some Muslims believe using wind and stringed instruments violates religious teaching. The trio's music is surprisingly rich, with layers of tonal beats driven by electronic rhythms and multitiered vocal tracks. Native Deen's fan base is almost exclusively Muslim although they say they would like someday to expand their reach. The group is working on their first collection of songs and is trying to get a recording contract.

Hip-hop music with a twist—that conforms to Muslim guidelines. If you didn't know better, Native Deen sounds a lot like many other religious performers trying to get their "big break" in the music industry. The difference is what their religion teaches about God and life. Ever since the terrorist attacks on the World Trade Center and the Pentagon, as well as the wars in Afghanistan and Iraq, a lot of people have had questions about what Muslims believe and why they believe it.

The History of Islam

Islam originated in what is now Saudi Arabia and was started by a man named Muhammad. It's the youngest of the major world religions, and an estimated one out of every six people on the face of this planet is a follower of Islam.

Muhammad was born in AD 570 to a prominent family in the Arabian city of Mecca. His family belonged to the Arabian tribe of Quraysh, which controlled the city of Mecca. This was a very important city in the ancient world economically. Because of its location, it served as a resting place for caravans. It was also important religiously because the Ka'bah was located there. The Ka'bah was built like a cube, and at the time Muhammad lived it contained 630 deities (gods). Each deity had been handpicked by an Arabian tribe, who then came to Mecca each year to worship it.

Unfortunately, Muhammad's childhood was filled with tragedy. His father died a few days before he was born and his mother died when he was only six years old. He then went to live with his grandfather, who died when Muhammad was nine years old. Finally he went to live with his uncle, Abu Talid, who owned large flocks of animals and ran caravans. Eventually Muhammad graduated from herding flocks and became involved in the caravan business, traveling with his uncle to Persia and Syria. Many scholars believe that it was during these times of traveling that Muhammad began to develop his ideas about monotheism (one God) from a variety of people whom he encountered on the road.

In the caravan trade Muhammad worked for a wealthy widow named Khadija. In time they fell in love and married, even though Khadija was fifteen years older than Muhammad (she was forty and he was twenty-five). They had several children and lived happily together.

It was the practice of those who were spiritually oriented to retreat each year and spend time in solitude. Muhammad observed this custom for a number of years in a cave on Mount Hira. It was in this cave, at the age of forty, that Muhammad received his first revelation from the angel Gabriel. According to Muhammad, the angel gave him the following command of God in a dream: "Read in the name of thy Lord who created, who created man of blood coagulated. Read! Thy Lord is the most beneficent, who taught by the pen, taught that what they knew not unto men."[2]

This was the first in a series of revelations Muhammad received and eventually compiled into Islam's sacred scripture, the Qur'an, meaning "the reciting" or "the reading." The Qur'an (Koran) is Muhammad's reciting of the revelations given to him because he couldn't read or write.

Muhammad was worried at first and began to have doubts about the origins of the new revelations. He even began to wonder if he had been possessed by *jinn* (demons). Arabic folklore taught that these supernatural beings influenced human affairs and could take the form of animals or humans. But Muhammad's wife Khadija reassured him that his visions were from God and that he should teach others what had been revealed to him.

Muhammad began to develop quite a following as he taught about monotheism in the streets and marketplace. Muhammad hated the immorality and idolatry of those who lived in Mecca or came there to trade. He began to get pressure from leaders in his own tribe to stop his teaching about one God. He was not only a threat to their polytheistic religion (many gods), but, more importantly, he was becoming a hazard to their economy as well because they profited from tribes making their pilgrimages to the Ka'bah. But Muhammad wouldn't stop his teaching. Finally, in 622, Muhammad was forced to leave Mecca and go to the city of Yathrib (now called

Medina). Muslims today consider the year of Muhammad's flight to
Yathrib—known as a "series of migrations" or the Hijrah (can also
be spelled Hegira)—as the beginning of the Muslim calendar.
Muhammad put together a vast army to conquer the world for
Allah. He and his army first carried out several successful sieges and
military victories against Mecca. They also made treaties with the
Quraysh tribe. Finally, in 630, Muhammad and his army took control of Mecca without a struggle. When he entered the city, he personally destroyed all the idols in the Ka'bah, except one. Muhammad
kept the Black Stone, a sacred meteorite that had been enshrined
there. He then declared the Ka'bah to be the most holy shrine in
Islam. Ever since that time, it has been the spot toward which all
devout Muslims direct their prayers.

Amazingly, within a year of Mecca's submission to Muhammad,
he was able to bring together every tribe on the Arabian Peninsula
under the religion of Islam. Muhammad died on June 8, 632.

What Do Muslims Believe?

The word *Islam* is related to the Arabic word for "peace" but is
properly translated as "submission" (to Allah, the God of
Muhammad). A *Muslim* is a believer in Muhammad's religion of Islam,
and the name means "one who lives his life according to God's will."

Islam in its original meaning is the primary act of self-surrender—
an act of choice whereby a person places his or her destiny in the
hands of Allah and submits to Allah's authority. The very word *Muslim*
means "one who has submitted himself to God." The kind of peace
offered such a person is expressed by the Arabic word *Salima*, which
means to be safe, unharmed, secure, or intact.[3]

The religion of Islam can be separated into beliefs (*iman*) and
duties or obligations (*deen*).

Beliefs

The six major beliefs or doctrines that every Muslim is expected
to believe are:

1. *God.* A core belief of Islam is that there is only one true God
(Allah) and there's not to be any partner associated with him. This is
why the Christian doctrine of the Trinity is offensive to a Muslim. If
you associate a partner with Allah, you commit the sin of *ishrak* (or
shirk) for which the Qur'an says there is no forgiveness (Sura 4:48).

2. *Angels.* In between Allah and humanity there's a pecking

order of angels filling in the gap. Gabriel has the highest rank, followed by the rest of the angels. There are two angels assigned to each man and woman: one to record all their good deeds and one to record the bad things. At the bottom of this hierarchy are the jinn, where the word *genie* comes from. Muslims believe that jinn are usually bad, can possess people, and were created by fire. Sounds a lot like demons!

3. *Holy Books.* Muslims believe that books of divine revelation were given to four of the higher-ranking prophets. The Torah, or Tawrat, was given to Moses (the Pentateuch); the Zabur to David (Psalms); the Injil to Jesus (Gospel); and the Qur'an to Muhammad. Because Muslims believe that Christians and Jews corrupted their Scriptures, only the Qur'an has been preserved in its uncorrupted state and, therefore, is Allah's final word to humanity.

4. *Prophets.* The Qur'an teaches that a prophet has been sent by God to every nation. Tradition says that 124,000 have been sent. Most of these are not named, but many biblical characters are on the prophets list, including Adam, Noah, Abraham, Moses, David, Solomon, Jonah, John the Baptist, and Jesus. Each prophet was given for a particular age, except Muhammad—he was the only one given for all time. Muslims consider him to be the "Seal of the Prophets."

5. *The Day of Judgment.* This is a critical area of belief for a Muslim. The Qur'an teaches that there will be a day when everyone will stand before Allah in judgment. On that day each person's deeds will be weighed on the scales (Sura 23.102f). "Then, when one blast is sounded on the Trumpet, and the earth is moved, and its mountains, and they are crushed to powder at one stroke—on that day shall ye be brought to Judgment: not an act of yours that ye hide will be hidden" (Sura 69:13–15, 18). If your good deeds outweigh your bad ones, you'll go to paradise. If your bad deeds outweigh your good ones, you'll be sent to hell.

The Islamic idea of paradise is very sensual and macho. Women do not have much to look forward to. Men who make it to paradise will recline on rich carpets and soft couches while downing cups of exotic drink they receive from maidens of paradise (*huris*). "They are virgin-pure and undefiled, with big, lustrous eyes" (Sura 88.8ff and 56.8–38).

Even though the Qur'an puts a lot of emphasis on ghastly punishments and sensual rewards, still the most devoted Muslim can never be confident of paradise. One of the seventeen major sins of

Islam is to "feel safe from the wrath of Allah." Even the promise that "the blessed shall dwell in paradise" is toned down by the additional words "unless Allah ordains otherwise" (Sura 11.108).

6. *Predestination.* Allah has already decided what you will get; he has determined what he pleases. No one can ever change his ruling. This is also known as *kismet*, the doctrine of fate. The most common Islamic phrase comes from this belief: "If it is Allah's will."

Duties

The five duties of Islam, also called the Five Pillars, are:

1. *Recite the Shahadah.* To become a Muslim, all you have to do is say the shahadah with sincerity. The word *shahadah* means "to bear witness." The words of the shahadah that must be recited are: "I bear witness that there is no God but Allah and that Muhammad is His messenger."

2. *Pray (Salat).* Muslims are required to say seventeen cycles (*rak'a*) of prayer every day. Generally these cycles are spread out over five times of prayer per day: daybreak, noon, midafternoon, after sunset, and early evening (two hours after sunset). They must wash themselves in the approved way before prayer, which is called absolution; kneel or bow; and pray in a group or individually. Muslims are also required to pray facing toward the holy city of Mecca.

3. *Give Alms (Zakat).* Islamic law requires that followers give one-fortieth of their income (2.5 percent). This money goes mainly to the poor, the sick, orphans, and widows.

4. *Fast (Sawm).* Muslims are required to fast for the entire month of Ramadan (the ninth month of the Islamic calendar) to commemorate when Muhammad received the Qur'an. They must give up eating, drinking, smoking, and sexual relations during daylight hours. After the sun goes down, Muslims are allowed to participate in all these things again until sunrise. Many Muslims eat two meals a day during Ramadan—one just before sunrise and one shortly after sunset.

5. *Pilgrimage to Mecca (Hajj).* This trip is a requirement of all Muslims at least once in their lifetime—as long as the person has the money and is healthy enough to make the trip. All status or class distinctions are eliminated during the Hajj because all pilgrims are required to wear a white garment called an *ihram.* The pilgrimage usually takes more than a

week because it also involves visiting several sacred sites. Once the pilgrims complete the pilgrimage, they earn the right to be called a Hajj.

These obligations or duties for Muslims are not only believed to be essentially good, but when they practice them, they're building up a stockpile of positive points or merit. Then on the Day of Judgment, these positive points earned while carrying out these duties will be taken into account.

Some people have also added a sixth duty to this list: "holy struggle" or *jihad*. The term *jihad* actually means "struggle" rather than "war," although physical combat is without a doubt part of the concept. The Qur'an and the Sunna both talk a lot about warfare. In his book *The Quranic Concept of War*, Pakistani Brigadier S. K. Malik, a devoted Muslim, explains: "The Holy Qur'an has given a comprehensive treatment to its concept of war. The Book defines and determines all aspects of the use of 'force' in interstate relations . . . . The Book also spells out a unique and distinctive concept of strategy, and prescribes its own rules and principles for the conduct of war."[4]

Keep in mind that there are specific restrictions on who can declare jihad and when and why. It's also very important to note that jihad also includes striving against one's own evil desires as well as defending the Islamic faith in ways other than combat—practices that are rarely mentioned by some of the more militant Islamic groups who have been complaining for quite awhile that jihad—in the militaristic meaning—is the "neglected duty."[5]

The Divisions of Islam

Before Muhammad died, he failed to appoint someone to serve as the first *caliph* (successor). He claimed to be God's last messenger on earth. This caused many arguments among Muhammad's followers and eventually caused Islam to break into two major divisions: Sunni and Shi'ite.

Sunni

The Sunni (orthodox) Muslims insisted that any early believer could be elected as Muhammad's successor. Sunnis also emphasize the authority of the holy writings, including the Qur'an and the Sunna ("custom," from where they get their name). The Sunna includes the Hadith, which contains the conduct and sayings of Muhammad and his companions. Sunnis think there should be a separation between religious and civil authorities, while the Shi'ites believe that the religious authorities should exercise both political and religious power. Most Muslims today are Sunni.

Shi'ite

Shi'ite Muslims (about 15 percent of all Muslims) believe that only direct descendants of Muhammad can inherit the position of successor. They accept a doctrine focused on a leader figure known as the *Inman,* through whom God speaks. The Inman is a religious leader, regarded as sinless, who has a direct lineage to Ali, the cousin of Muhammad. The Inman would be the Muslim equivalent to the Catholic pope. In the ninth century the Twelfth Inman became hidden and the new source of authority became the *ulama,* who see themselves collectively as representing the hidden Inman. Much like Christians wait for the Second Coming of Jesus Christ, Shi'ite Muslims wait for the return of the Twelfth Inman. They are more authority driven rather than consensus seeking, as are the Sunni.

Splinter Groups

Besides these two major divisions of Islam, three smaller splinter groups exist: Sufi, Taliban, and the Nation of Islam.

Sufi. These are the mystics of Islam. The Sufis are individuals who look for union with God through contemplation, prayer, and asceticism (fasting, going without sleep, and tolerating rough conditions).

Taliban. In the late 1970s, when Russia invaded Afghanistan, many people were sent to refugee camps in Pakistan. Some of the students at this time began to interpret Islamic law in an extreme way. They were called "students of the Islamic knowledge movement" or *Talibs.* The Taliban ("Allah's Army") started to grow, and on September 27, 1996, they took over the capital of Afghanistan. The Taliban members ran around the city streets with whips, beating anyone they thought was not living up to the Taliban's Islamic standards. Though they took over the capital in 1996, Pakistan is the only other country that recognizes them as rulers. The Taliban version of Islamic law allows them to administer justice arbitrarily, such as amputating the arm of a thief or stoning a woman who is walking down the street without a male from her family. The Taliban also has chosen to protect international terrorist Osama bin Laden, the mastermind behind the attacks against the U.S. on September 11, 2001.

Nation of Islam. In the 1930s, W. D. Fard Muhammad began the

Black Muslim movement, which focused on the idea of black superiority. He said that the first humans were black and that a black scientist created white people as a result of an experiment. He also taught that white people oppressed black people and that Christianity should be rejected because it is the main religion of white people. W. D. Fard trained a younger man—Elijah Muhammad—to be a leader. In the 1960s, this leader, now called Malcolm X, decided that the idea of hating people should be changed. Unfortunately, some people opposed his idea and assassinated him. Their current leader is Louis Farrakhan, who believes the black race is better than the white. Some have even called his religion "Farrakhanism." Followers of the Nation of Islam and Farrakhan adhere to the moral law of traditional Islam, but they also believe that W. D. Fard Muhammad was god (Allah) in the flesh and his successor, Elijah Muhammad, was his prophet. On judgment day, they believe all the gods (who are black) will destroy the "devil" white race and establish paradise on earth. This paradise will be called "The Nation of Islam."

There is one more important distinction we need to quickly examine: the difference between Islam in the West and Islam in the East. In the West, Islam projects a "user-friendly" image—a religion that is tolerant, just, and filled with love. In the East, however, it has been historically and is currently being practiced more as a political religion. Most religious leaders in Islamic countries believe that all of society must submit to Islamic law if Islam is to be correctly practiced. This means that everyone must conform or suffer serious consequences. There is continuing persecution of Christians in Muslim countries—including rape and murder.

Key Differences between Islam and Christianity

There are many significant differences between what Muslims and Christians believe. Here are some of the important ones.

- Muslims believe there is only one God—Allah. There are to be no partners associated with God. Christians believe in the three persons of the Trinity who are coeternally God, revealed in the Bible as Father, Son, and Holy Spirit (Matt. 3:13–17; 28:19; 2 Cor. 13:14).
- Islam teaches that people are basically good by nature. Christianity says that people are sinful by nature (Rom. 3:12; Eph. 5:8–10).

- Muslims believe that sin is mainly rejecting the right guidance. Sin is serious stuff in Christianity. So serious that it causes spiritual death (Rom. 6:23). It is moral rebellion against a holy God that results in separation from Him. This relationship can only be restored through the shed blood of Jesus Christ (1 Pet. 3:18).

- Muslims believe that salvation is based on human effort and may be gained by having your good deeds outweigh your bad deeds. In Christianity, salvation cannot be earned. It is the free gift of God—a result of His grace and mercy (Eph. 2:8–9). Jesus Christ made this possible by dying for our sins (Rom. 5:8; 1 Cor. 15:3–4).

- Islam teaches that Jesus was a major prophet, below Muhammad, and not God. To even call Him the Son of God is considered blasphemy. Although Muslims do believe in Jesus' virgin birth and that He performed miracles, Christians believe that Jesus is the one and only Son of God, the Savior, the one who died and rose again (Rom. 5:1; 1 Tim. 2:5).

- Muslims believe that the Bible has been corrupted and that the Qur'an is the final word of God. Christians believe that the Bible is authentic, divinely inspired, and the final authority in all matters of truth and faith (2 Tim. 3:16).

- Islam teaches that Jesus did not die on the cross. Instead, He ascended into heaven and Judas actually died in His place on the cross. Muslims believe that it is disrespectful to think that God would allow one of His major prophets to be crucified.

  Christianity, on the other hand, teaches that Jesus died a physical death as our substitute—He died our death. He voluntarily gave His life for us (John 6:51; 10:11–17). After three days, Jesus rose from the grave in bodily form and appeared to hundreds of people (1 Cor. 15). God's main reason for sending Jesus into the world was to die on the cross for our sins (John 3:16; Rom. 8:3; 2 Cor. 5:21; 1 Pet. 1:19–20). The end result of Jesus' death was not dishonor but the highest exaltation (Acts 2:29–33; 5:30–31; Phil. 2:8–11).

Think about It

1. What do you think the attraction is for someone to become a Muslim? What's the appeal?

2. How does Islam appear to be like Christianity?

3. If you have the opportunity to talk with a Muslim about your relationship with Christ, remember the following things:

- Respect them and their beliefs.

- Refer to the Bible frequently and let them know that's where you find the support for your faith. Handle the Bible with respect. Remember, Muslims treat the Qur'an with so much respect that no other book in their house is allowed to be higher than it.

- Meet and talk with them individually not in a group. They will be much more honest with their doubts about Islam when they are alone.

- Refer to Jesus as often as possible. Muslims need to see that Christianity is not a religion but a relationship with the living God made possible by Jesus' death on the cross and His resurrection.

Chapter Four

Buddhism

One of the most influential Buddhists in modern times was the late Bruce Lee, who introduced martial arts (or Kung Fu) to Hollywood in the 1960s and single-handedly started the whole Kung Fu excitement in the United States. Even though Lee popularized martial arts through his movies and TV show, its development is attributed to the Indian monk Bodhidharma, who came to China to start Zen Buddhism. Reportedly, he meditated for seven years in the Shaolin Buddhist temple, which is considered to be the birthplace of Kung Fu.

Actor Richard Gere is the most well-known Buddhist in the United States, and he has been instrumental in spreading Buddhism to the West. He is an active supporter of the Dalai Lama and provided the main financial support (together with other Hollywood celebrities such as Harrison Ford and Sharon Stone) for the Dalai Lama to visit America to give lectures on Buddhism to the public. Gere was formerly married to model Cindy Crawford—who said she got sick and tired of Buddhist rituals and sought divorce from Gere.

Other Buddhist celebrities include actor and martial arts expert Steven Segal; actor Patrick Duffy, who says that he belongs to the Nichiren Shoshu sect (a "name it and claim it" form of Buddhism) and recites *om mani padme* at least once a day; actor Harrison Ford, who was instrumental in making the film *Seven Years in Tibet,* although he took no direct role in the movie about the young Dalai Lama; and Grammy-award-winning singer Tina Turner, who plans to spread the words of Dharma after she retires from her singing career (also a follower of the Nichiren Shoshu). Singer Joan Baez and NBA coach Phil Jackson of the world champion LA Lakers practice Zen

Buddhism. In an interview Jackson said, "Zen is a particular way of looking at life. It's the moment, being in the present. Buddhism is compassionate and Christianity is based on love. So those two things coordinate very well together."[1]

Even though I am a huge Lakers fan and have great respect for Phil Jackson as a coach, I have to disagree with him about the compatibility of Buddhism and Christianity. While there may be some common ground with things like living a moral life, compassion for the poor and self-discipline as a virtue to pursue, there are some tremendous differences in essential beliefs that contradict each other.

The Origins of Buddhism

Buddhism evolved from Hinduism and was founded by Siddhartha Gautama during the sixth century BC. He was born the son of a wealthy and powerful ruler in the town of Kapilavastu, an area that is now part of Nepal. Legend holds that an old sage told Siddhartha's father that his son would grow up to become one of the greatest rulers in the world. However, the old sage also predicted that if Siddhartha ever saw four things—sickness, old age, death, and a monk who had renounced the world—the boy would give up his earthly rule and find a way of salvation for all humanity.

The father was eager to protect his son and make sure he'd become a great ruler. An awesome palace was built, and Siddhartha was kept isolated from the world. He lived in luxury and got anything he wanted. Eventually he married a beautiful girl named Yasodhara, and they had son. But one day Siddhartha ventured outside the royal estate and ended up seeing all four kinds of suffering. The journey shocked him and forever changed his life. Siddhartha became disillusioned with his wealth and was consumed with the issue of suffering.

As a result of this experience, Siddhartha, at age twenty-nine, left his life of luxury and his family. His followers call this the Great Renunciation. Siddhartha was determined to eliminate suffering, solve the riddle of life, and find enlightenment. He started his search with the Hindu religion but found no satisfaction there. Then Siddhartha tried asceticism—totally giving up the comforts of life. He subjected himself to intense physical disciplines and self-denial, but spiritual answers continued to escape him. He practically starved himself and almost drowned while trying to bathe in a river because he was so weak. Still he found no happiness.

Siddhartha then ate some food, walked to the city of Bodh Gaya, and sat by the edge of a river under a fig tree. He vowed that he would not move until he found what he was searching for. He then went into a deep state of meditation. Once again, legend holds that Siddhartha was severely tempted by Mara, the evil one. After a period of time (some say one night; others, up to forty-nine days), he attained enlightenment and became the Buddha, which means "the enlightened one." Bodh Gaya is now the location of the Mahabodhi ("great enlightenment") Temple—the holiest site in the Buddhist world.

After this experience, Buddha traveled to teach about the meaning of life and his way to nirvana. He called his path to enlightenment the Middle Way because it avoided the extremes of wealth and self-denial. Buddha gave his first message—which has become known as the Four Noble Truths—in a place called Deer Park. These became the basic "road map" to help followers avoid obstacles that keep them from understanding their true nature and identity. It explained the steps—the same ones Buddha took—to reaching the experience of nirvana, the ultimate reality.

What Is Buddhism?

Although Buddhism has evolved and expanded throughout the centuries, the fundamental beliefs have remained unchanged since the time of Buddha. These basic beliefs include the Four Noble Truths, first explained by Buddha in Deer Park:

1. *Life consists of suffering* (dukkha). Pain and suffering are part of life—from birth to death. Even death does not end suffering because of the cycle of rebirth, suffering, and death. Once nirvana is reached, an individual is released from the cycle of suffering.
2. *The cause of suffering is selfish desire (the principle of* anicca— *"no self").* People remain in this endless cycle because they are too attached to their physical comfort, wealth, status, and health. This is a result of their ignorance of reality.
3. *The cure for suffering is to eliminate all desire.* Because suffering is part of life and suffering is caused by selfish desires, once all cravings are removed, suffering ends.
4. *Following the Eightfold Path can eliminate desire.* Buddha taught these eight points for people to follow in order to escape from the cycle of death and rebirth. The points of the Eightfold Path can be grouped in three major sections:

1. Wisdom (*Panna*)
   • Right understanding
   • Right thought
2. Ethical Conduct (*Sila*)
   • Right speech
   • Right behavior
   • Right occupation
3. Mental Discipline (*Samadhi*)
   • Right effort
   • Right alertness
   • Right meditation

Although these attitudes and actions are to be developed simultaneously, not one step after another, the first two points are the foundation from which the other six points naturally follow. At the heart of this path is Wisdom—right understanding and thought. Achieving wisdom gives the ability to speak well about others, to obey Buddhism's moral commands, and to engage in an acceptable occupation that does not involve breaking any moral commands.

The moral commands, which are the source for ethical conduct (*sila*) and are to be abstained from, are:
• The taking of life (all forms, not only human)
• Stealing
• Immoral sexual behavior (monks must be celibate)
• Lying
• The taking of intoxicants (drugs, alcohol)

While the sila (ethical conduct) deals with actions, the samadhi (mental discipline) deals with attitudes. It is defined as a deep state of consciousness "in which all sense of personal identity ceases."[2] These three points of samadhi supposedly enable individuals to keep evil thoughts out of their minds, stay aware of events in their lives, and enable them, through meditation, to get the pleasure of enlightenment.

Keep in mind that the number one priority for Buddha was to eliminate the cause of suffering. His ultimate goal was to help others become liberated from the cycle of death and rebirth by teaching them how to eliminate all desire and attachment to the things of this world as well as their belief in the illusionary self. By getting rid of any attachments to the world, individuals give the effects of karma nothing to grab on to, thereby ultimately releasing themselves from the realm of illusion and, at that moment of enlightenment, achieving the state of nirvana. This is the ultimate goal for a Buddhist—their equivalent of salvation. Buddha described nirvana (*Pali, nibbana*) as follows:

> There is a sphere which is neither earth, nor water, nor fire, nor air, which is not the sphere of the infinity of space, nor the sphere of the infinity of consciousness, the sphere of nothingness, the sphere of perception, or non-perception, which is neither this world, neither sun nor moon. I deny that it is coming or going, enduring, death, or birth. It is only the end of suffering.[3]

Buddha always maintained that his mission was to show others the way to escape the suffering of life, not to describe what one would find once he had been enlightened. In reality, one does not cease to exist when entering the state of nirvana because, as Buddha has reasoned, there never existed any person to be annihilated in the first place—"no self."

Major Forms of Buddhism

For about two hundred years Buddhism didn't spread beyond the borders of India. But King Ashoka (274–232 BC) changed all that. Ashoka was a warrior-king who became so disgusted by the bloodshed during one battle that he resolved to abandon all such fighting and became a Buddhist. From then on, King Ashoka dedicated himself and all his resources to spreading Buddhism. He recruited and sent out Buddhist missionaries to other parts of India, plus Thailand, Greece, Sri Lanka, Myanmar, Cyrene, Egypt, and Syria.

Around this same time a major split took place in Buddhism. The dividing factor was over the issue of enlightenment and whether it was accessible to only a select few or to everyone. *Hinayana* ("the lesser vehicle") Buddhists said enlightenment was only available to a committed few—monks, for example. Because of much criticism over the term "lesser vehicle," the Hinayanas changed their name to *Theravada* Buddhists, which means "the teaching of the elders." The group who said that enlightenment was available to everyone called themselves *Mahayana* or "the greater vehicle." These two forms of Buddhism also differed in whether a follower strives to become a *bodhisattva* or an *arahat*. With the Mahayana idea of bodhisattva, after one attains enlightenment, he or she refuses to enter nirvana because of great compassion for all the people who have not yet reached enlightenment. The follower comes back to guide others along the right path. Buddhist monks who follow this "savior" path are called "bodhisattvas."

In the Theravada idea of arahat, there is more concern with one's own enlightenment than that of others'. The main concern is to make sure that enlightenment is attained by abandoning all deceptions of reality.

Mahayanas and Theravadas also have radically different views of Buddha and other aspects of Buddhism. Theravadas see Buddha as a man—a teacher—and not a god. Mahayanas, however, have elevated Buddha to a position of a "savior-god" for all people. Mahayana Buddhism is more popular because of this concept and is more influential in places such as Korea, Vietnam, Japan, Tibet, China, and Nepal.

Other differences between Theravada and Mahayana Buddhism include the following:

- Theravadas insist that there can only be one Buddha. Mahayanas believe there have been many appearances of the Buddha spirit.
- Theravadas teach that you can only achieve enlightenment through your own individual effort. Mahayanas teach that not only can the bodhisattvas help you along the path, they can also transfer some of their own good karma to those who are seeking.

A popular form of Mahayana Buddhism in the West is *Zen*—a discipline that uses meditation as the means to reach enlightenment (reaching satori). Those who teach Zen stress the proverb of the Buddha: "Look within, you are the Buddha." This form of Buddhism has become popular with many in the West, including celebrities and entertainers as mentioned at the beginning of this chapter.

There is also a third major form of Buddhism known as *Vajrayana* or *Tantra*. Vajrayana Buddhism comes from a form of Hinduism called tantra, which puts emphasis on using occultic techniques for increasing spiritual power. Vajrayana Buddhism is the main religion in Tibet, from where the Dalai Lama comes. The Dalai Lama is the most recognizable living symbol of Buddhism in the world today and is also Tibet's exiled spiritual and political leader. Buddhists in Tibet believe that the Dalai Lama is the fourteenth reincarnation of Avalokiteshvara, the bodhisattva of compassion.

Finally, when trying to gain an understanding of Buddhism, you must also be aware that there is a distinction between the "folk" version of Buddhism and the "official" version. These two varieties of Buddhism are distinct from one another. Most people who practice the folk version know very little about the official version. Buddhists who practice the folk version are animistic—they attribute conscious life to nonliving objects or things in nature. They believe that spirits influence and control people's lives and that you must satisfy the spirits in order to gain success. Folk Buddhists also believe that you should seek the guidance of the spirits through various forms of divination.

The Buddhist Sacred Writings

Another issue in the split between Theravada and Mahayana Buddhism was over the sacred writings or scriptures. According to the Theravadas, the list of writings to be included was closed with the Pali Tripitaka. *Pali* describes the language it was written in and the *Tripitaka* (also spelled *Tipitaka*) means the "three baskets" of teachings: philosophical teachings, Buddha's sermons, and rules for monks. The Tripitaka is about seventy times the length of the Bible.

In contrast, the Mahayanas believed the list of writings stayed open. They included scripture writings from Tibetan, Indian, Chinese, and Japanese sources. The Lotus Sutra (Saddharma-pundarika) and the Perfection of Wisdom (Prajna-paramita), which also include the Heart and Diamond Sutras, are some of the more popular Mahayana scriptures.

The sacred scriptures of Vajrayana Buddhism are the Tanjur (225 volumes) and the Kanjur (108 volumes).

Differences between Buddhism and Hinduism

Even though there are similarities between Buddhism and Hinduism, there are still some very distinct differences. Some teachings of Buddha were so different that Hindu Brahmin priests rejected them as blasphemy. This included things like Buddha saying that the Hindu Vedas and the Upanishads were not divine writings and they could not help anyone find the path to nirvana. Buddha taught that people had no soul (*atman*), which is part of the Brahman (world soul); plus, he denied that the present world is unreal (*maya*).

Buddha emphasized ethics over ritual by rejecting the concept of the Hindu system of sacrifice and the Brahmin priesthood. He taught that enlightenment was available to anyone—including women—and rejected the caste system (social order). Buddha also taught that all the indifferent Hindu gods and goddesses were basically not necessary in the pursuit of enlightenment. Yet Buddha did include into his teachings two highly developed Hindu skills: meditation and yoga.

Regarding reincarnation, Hinduism envisions an individual soul that is the same from lifetime to lifetime. According to Buddhism, however, no individual self (soul) exists from one lifetime to the next through the cycle of reincarnation. Instead, every individual is made up of five "aggregates," called *skandhas*. This collective group includes the physical body, emotions, perception, will, and consciousness. When death occurs, this collective group is taken apart—dismantled, as one might take apart an engine. And just as an engine doesn't function after being taken apart piece by piece, neither does the skandhas exist after death. Buddha also taught that an individual could be reborn as a human, an animal, a demon, a hungry ghost, or even as a Hindu god.

Key Differences between Buddhism and Christianity

There are many significant differences between what Buddhists and Christians believe. Here are some of the important ones.

- Buddhists do not believe in a personal God. Theravada Buddhists believe in nirvana, an abstract void. Mahayana Buddhists also believe in nirvana and in an undifferentiated Buddha spirit. Christians believe in a personal God who is self-existent, all-powerful, all-knowing, and never changing (Job 42:1–6; Ps. 115:3; Mal. 3:6; Matt. 19:26).

- Buddha claimed to point the way to escape suffering and achieve enlightenment. Jesus said He was the way to salvation and eternal life (John 14:6; 5:25).

- Mahayana Buddhists view the physical world as an illusion to be escaped. The Bible teaches that Jesus created the universe, and He called it good (Gen. 1:31; John 1:3).

- The bodhisattvas (Mahayana Buddhists) had to overcome their own sin (self, ignorance, etc.) during the process of being reincarnated through numerous lifetimes. Yet from the very beginning Jesus was without sin. He did not have to go through some kind of process to make Himself sinless (Matt. 27:4; Luke 23:41; 2 Cor. 5:21; Heb. 4:15). For the Christian, salvation comes only through faith in what Christ has done for us (Acts 4:12; Eph. 2:8–9).

- Buddha taught that the way to eliminate suffering was by eliminating desire (Theravada Buddhism). Jesus' answer to end suffering is not to eliminate all desire but to have the right desire (Matt. 5:6). The Bible does talk about "evil desires" (James 1:13–15) that come from within a person, and these passions (or appetites) tend to get out of control. When we give in to these temptations, we sin. The result of sin is spiritual suffering and death (Rom. 6:23).
- Buddha taught that we must learn to master ourselves. The Bible teaches that without God we do not have the strength to control our desires. But through Christ we have strength to do all things (Phil. 4:13) and live successfully.
- Buddhists believe that Jesus was a good teacher but less important than the Buddha. Christians believe that Jesus is the unique Son of God who died for the sins of humanity (Matt. 14:33; John 1:34; Rom. 5:6–8).

Think about It

1. What do others at your school think about Buddhism? Do you think their opinion is based on accurate information?

2. If you could share with someone only one specific difference between Buddhism and Christianity, what would it be and why?

3. If you have the opportunity to talk with a Buddhist about your relationship with Christ, remember the following things:

- Be aware that when someone claims to be a Buddhist, he or she can be referring to one of several different forms of Buddhism, including the "folk" version, which is animistic.
- Talk about the common ground you share, such as living a moral life, the importance of self-discipline, and the importance of meditation and prayer. Make sure, however, that you explain how Christians and Buddhists approach these concepts. At some point you should also point out how the basic beliefs of both religions are very different and why.
- Explain that the Christian God is personal, loving, and has emotions.
- Focus on the uniqueness of Jesus. Challenge the person to study the teachings of Jesus from the New Testament. Remind him or her that salvation is not based on human effort; it's a gift from God.

- If a Buddhist rejects your message about Jesus, ask why. It might be because of a different perspective or misunderstanding. Most Buddhists have never really heard a clear presentation of the God's love, forgiveness, and acceptance.
- Clearly explain sin and forgiveness.

Chapter Five

Hinduism

George Harrison was known as the quiet Beatle. Unassuming and mysterious, lead guitarist Harrison was always the most elusive of the Fab Four. He wasn't like John, the intellectual rebel; or like Ringo, the lovable mascot; or like Paul, the cute romantic. He was the first Beatle to embrace sitars, meditation, and Eastern religion. Harrison rejected his Catholic roots to explore Indian spirituality. Eventually he became a Hare Krishna, a faction of Hinduism. He once told a friend that he would give up everything if he could be a monk who walks from one side of India to another. After the Beatles broke up, Harrison had a number-one single with a tune about the Hindu god Krishna entitled "My Sweet Lord."

Harrison made several pilgrimages to India in his lifelong search to know his god. When his son was born, he and his wife Olivia named him Dhani—Hindu for "rich man." After Harrison's death at age fifty-eight from cancer, his ashes were scattered on the waters of two of India's most sacred rivers, the Ganges and the Yamuna, continuing a tradition dating back thousands of years. For Hindus, nothing is holier than dying by the bank of the Ganges—and if that's not possible, second-best is sprinkling one's ashes on its waters. The singer's family even asked his fans to join them in a minute's meditation at the time of the immersion "in honor of George's journey."

According to the tenets of Hinduism, followed by the Krishna movement, the immersion or scattering of ashes on the sacred river is a symbol of the soul's journey toward eternal consciousness. Hindus believe that if their ashes are sprinkled in the Ganges, the soul achieves salvation. From India's leaders, such as Gandhi and Nehru, to ordinary citizens, the last rites of millions of Hindus have taken place along the Ganges and the Yamuna. The best time to conduct the ceremony is just before dawn, at the start of a new day. And the holiest site for cremation or the immersion of ashes is in the city of Varanasi, one of the oldest in the world. If you happen to be lucky enough to die there, it releases you from the cycle of death and rebirth.

On any given day, thousands of Hindus arrive in the city to wash by the river and cleanse their souls. Many others arrive simply to die—patiently waiting by the river's edge. Another sacred site is in the city of Allahabad—where the Ganges and Yamuna rivers join together.

As a strong believer in the Krishna faction, George Harrison would have been familiar with the ritual of immersion. But he also had an older, more profound link with the Ganges. It runs through the retreat of a Hindu spiritual guru, Maharishi Mahesh Yogi, in the Himalayan town of Rishikesh, where Harrison had his first brush with Hinduism. Here, along the clear waters of the Ganges rapids, he began his spiritual discovery of Eastern mysticism, which eventually led him to his involvement with the Krishna movement.

Many other celebrities have embraced Hinduism, including Madonna. In her video for the song "Music," she morphed into a six-armed Hinduesque figure. At the 1998 VH1 awards, she dressed as a Hindu priestess, and in her video for "Frozen," she wore Hindu body art (mendhi). But probably the most well-known Hindu of all was Mahatma Ghandi.

While George Harrison, Madonna, and Mahatma Ghandi have all influenced great numbers of people throughout the world, their own lives were influenced by a confusing religion of contradictions.

The History of Hinduism

Hinduism is more than 4,000 years old and has changed significantly throughout history. It actually started in the Indus Valley, which is modern-day Pakistan. The Indus Valley civilization, populated by Dravidians, was a mercantile and agricultural society that used a pictorial language that even scholars today have been unable to completely decode. They had a polytheistic (belief in many gods) fertility religion. Around 2000 BC Aryans (nothing to do with the Nazi "master race") invaded from the Northwest and conquered the people of the Indus Valley.

Because the Aryans were also polytheistic, some of the most popular Dravidian gods received new Aryan names, though they retained their old functions. Between 2000 and 700 BC the hymns, mythic stories, prayers, and chants of the Aryans were written down in the Vedas, Aranyakas, and Upanishads, collectively known as the Vedic literature. Hindus consider these volumes to be supernaturally inspired and sacred, just like Christians feel about the Bible.

The early Hindus were clearly polytheistic, devoted to rituals and sacrifices. Later they moved toward pantheism, the belief that God didn't create the world; rather, God *is* the world and everything in it. Even though early Hindu writings mentioned many gods, later Vedic literature set as the highest goal union with Brahma—the "impersonal absolute." Brahmins, the priests of Brahma, carried out ritual duties for the common people to satisfy the many gods, which early Vedic writings required. Because the Brahmins were the keepers of the higher truths of their pantheistic religion, they grew increasingly powerful and eventually became the highest social class.

Around 500 BC the Hindu scriptures were expanded to establish Varna—a rigid caste system or social order. One song describes how four social groups of people came from the head, arms, thighs, and feet of Brahma—the creator god. The four social groups were the priests (Brahmins), the nobles and warriors (Kshatriyas), the artisans and merchants (Vaisyas), and the slaves (Shudras). Each social group was then subdivided into hundreds of smaller groups, arranged in order of rank. The only ones who could get all the benefits that the Hindu religion had to offer were the priests, the nobles and warriors, and the artisans and merchants. The slaves were not allowed to hear the Vedas or to use them to try and find salvation.

Yet there was one group of people considered even lower than the slaves: the Untouchables. Until the twentieth century, they were considered so low that they were completely outside the social group system, essentially considered subhuman. Untouchables were deprived of property, education, and basic human dignity. They always had the dirtiest jobs, ate rotten food and drank polluted water, wore rags for clothes, and oftentimes watched their children die of starvation. The Indian government officially outlawed discrimination against Untouchables when India became a nation in 1947. Christian missionaries played a key role in challenging this religious social order and helping to get the laws changed. Unfortunately, today in India there are still many villages where Untouchables are outcasts.

What Is Hinduism?

Hinduism is a varied group of many religions that interact with one another. Even though there are ideas that contradict each other, they're all acceptable in Hinduism because all reality is seen as "one." As a Hindu, a follower can choose to believe in no god, one god, or many gods! Hindus are tolerant of other religious beliefs as long as the individual is a genuine follower of a valid religion. That's because they believe that many religions teach the way to salvation, with Hinduism simply being one of them.

Hinduism is also unique among religions in the world because it doesn't have a founder, a headquarters, or even a central person in charge, plus there are many holy books within their religious system. It's also one of the few religions that promotes the worship of animals. Orthodox Hindus think peacocks and cattle are sacred and will not allow them to be killed under any circumstances. No cheeseburgers please!

Even though Hinduism is a massive religious system with countless entry points, there are some shared beliefs commonly accepted by Hindu believers. Most Hindus believe that:

- Many paths lead to Brahma.
- Brahma (the Absolute or Ultimate Reality) is both personal and impersonal. It's also visible in lots of different symbols of divine truth.
- There is a single god and lots and lots of individual deities to worship. Each deity is considered to be a useful form of Brahma—one of the three supreme gods in the Hindu triad and respected as the creator of the world. Hindus believe the earth is only supposed to last 2.16 billion years before it falls into ruin and Brahma must recreate it again. Krishna and Rama are incarnations of Vishnu, who is viewed as the preserver and power of inspiring love in the Hindu triad. Shiva, the third supreme god in the Hindu triad, is usually illustrated with four arms and surrounded by fire, and it represents the idea of destruction and creative force.
- The early collection of Hindu scriptures, or Vedas, is reliable and divinely inspired.
- Reality, or the physical world, is really an illusion and is able to hide the divine truth from all but the wisest of people.

- There are four disciplines, or yogas, that can lead to enlightenment: *janana,* which stresses meditation and commands the power of the mind; *bhakti,* which supports the path of one's love to God; *karma,* which involves service to others; and *raja,* combines elements of all three into a single ritual and includes "hatha yoga," which is supposed to help develop complete control over the body.
- Life has four objectives: righteousness, earthly wealth and success, pleasure, and spiritual freedom.

To further understand Hinduism, you must be familiar with two foundational concepts that nearly all Hindus believe.

1. *Reincarnation* is about recycling the soul. It's the belief that a person's eternal and uncreated soul (*atman*) must be frequently recycled into different bodies. Souls may be reincarnated as plants, animals, and even nonliving objects in some forms of Hinduism. Reincarnation is the process that runs a Hindu's soul through the great wheel of *samsara* for the thousands or millions of lives (all full of misery) that each must undergo before reaching *moksha*—freedom from suffering and coming together with the infinite. Samsara is the progression of accumulated birth, in which the thoughts and deeds of past lives are addressed and resolved in subsequent lives. Many Hindus believe that true freedom from this karma-driven cycle is next to impossible.

2. *Karma* ("action") is an impartial force, similar to the law of cause and effect. It's not filtered through a supreme being and takes no sides. It affects even the smallest aspects of human life. For the Hindu, after your soul is reincarnated in another body, you start paying for the bad things you did in a previous existence. It's the law of moral consequences, or "you pay for what you do." Karma demands payment for misdeeds, yet there is no personal God to receive payment!

Karma from a past life affects your present life, and karma from this life will decide your position in the next life. With any luck, after many lives you will find that the good you have done outweighs the bad, in which case there is hope of nirvana (not the band or the ice cream), where all consciousness ends and you return to the fundamental "One" that underlies or embraces everything in the universe. There is no eternal life or "you."

The Bible completely contradicts the ideas of reincarnation and karma. In Hinduism, the soul is eternal and uncreated. It's also free, unlimited, and perfect, and eventually every soul will become conscious of its divine nature—no matter how many lives it takes. The Bible teaches that each person lives and dies only once and after that comes judgment (John 5:17–30; 1 Cor. 15; Heb. 9:27).

The ultimate goal and challenge for the Hindu is for the soul to escape the trap of samsara and be reunited with Brahma—Ultimate Reality. There are only three paths to freedom and enlightenment (*moksha*) that a Hindu can take: the way of works, the way of knowledge, and the way of devotion.

A person who follows the way of works (*dharma* or *karma marga*) must fulfill a very specific set of religious and social duties (action and ritual). He must follow his social order (caste) occupation, or eat certain foods and marry within his social order. However, the most important duty to fulfill is that of having a son who then can perform sacrificial and ritual acts, including making a sacrifice to his ancestors. If these duties are satisfied, the person following dharma may have the chance of attaining a better reincarnation the next time and ultimately, after maybe thousands of additional reincarnations, finally achieve enlightenment.

The way of knowledge and meditation (*jnana marga*) is a much more difficult path to follow. This way is open only to men in the highest social orders and includes self-renunciation and meditating on the pantheistic (God is everything) truth of Hinduism. Usually this road of knowledge includes the practice of yoga. Yoga is the effort to control your consciousness through bodily posture, breath control, and concentration. The goal is to reach a point where you understand experientially that your soul—your true self—is identical with Brahma. This is where the famous Hindu saying "I am Brahma" comes from.

The most popular way to try to achieve enlightenment is the path of devotion (*bhakti marga*). If you decide to follow this path, you have the option to choose any of the 330 million Hindu gods, goddesses, or demigods and zealously worship that specific god. Usually, most Hindus following this way end up worshipping Vishnu or Shiva. This way has great appeal to the lower classes (the vast majority of the Indian population) and offers a much easier path for their souls to progress to higher forms of birth through reincarnation, eventually reaching enlightenment. There are no strenuous yoga exercises to perform, nor is there need to be part of the intellectual elite or of a special social order.

By the mid-nineteenth century, Hindu ideas began to influence Western thinking. Writers such as Ralph Waldo Emerson and Henry David Thoreau steeped themselves in Hindu literature, which later influenced their own writings. Eventually, Swami Prabhavananda formed the Vedanta Society of Southern California. Vedanta played a major role in the New Age movement and claims to be friendly toward all religions. Teachers of Vedanta say that a Hindu "would find it easy to accept Christ as a divine incarnation and to worship Him unreservedly, exactly as he worships Krishna or another avatar ('savior') of his choice. But he cannot accept Christ as the only Son of God."[1]

Hinduism has entered mainstream culture of the United States in such a way that even certain ancient Vedantic ideas go unquestioned by millions of Americans. A good example of this is the Vedantic motto: All approaches to God are true and valid.

Key Differences between Hinduism and Christianity

There are many significant differences between what Hindus and Christians believe. Here are some of the important ones.

- Hindus do not believe in a personal God. Instead, they believe in Brahma, an abstract, formless eternal being. Christians believe that God is a personal, spiritual being found in three eternal persons: Father, Son, and Holy Spirit (Matt. 3:13–17; 28:19; 2 Cor. 13:14).
- The Hindu way to enlightenment is from humanity to God and is based on a person's own effort. The biblical way of salvation is just the opposite, going from God to humanity, and is a gift to be received through faith, based on God's grace (Eph. 2:8–9; 1 John 4:10).
- Hinduism offers at least three paths to enlightenment: the way of action and ritual, the way of knowledge and meditation, and the way of devotion. Christianity teaches that there is only one way to salvation: through Jesus Christ (John 14:6).
- Hinduism teaches that humanity's problem is ignorance; Christianity teaches that it's moral rebellion.
- In Hinduism, karma does not affect the relationship with Brahma. In Christianity, sin separates us from God because He is holy (Isa. 59:2).

- In Hinduism the morality, the law of karma, becomes like a law of nature, making forgiveness impossible and consequences inescapable. Because people can forgive and God is a person, God can forgive us for our sins. He has done this through Jesus Christ's death on the cross (Rom. 5:8; 6:23; 1 Pet. 3:18).

- In Hinduism the outcome of enlightenment and liberation is merging into the "Oneness" as the individual disappears. In Christianity the outcome of salvation is fulfillment and eternal fellowship with God through a loving relationship with Him (John 1:12).

Think about It

1. Have you noticed any Hindu beliefs showing up in movies, TV shows you watch, or music that you listen to? How about books you have read at school or for pleasure?

2. Do you know someone who is a practicing Hindu? Have you talked with them about your faith, and if so, what kind of questions came up?

3. If you have the opportunity to talk with a Hindu about your relationship with Christ, remember the following things:

- Ask questions about what the person believes, and listen carefully to the answers.

- Explain that the Christian God is personal and loving.

- Focus on who Jesus is and His offer of forgiveness. Challenge the person to study the teachings of Jesus from the New Testament.

Chapter Six

Mormonism

I t was a few days before Christmas and the post office was packed. The line circled the inside of the station like a human snake, then made its way out the door. I took my place in line, already dreading the long wait. I noticed two young men standing in front of me wearing dark pants, starched white shirts, ties, and an unmistakable name badge on their pockets. They were Mormon missionaries.

I suddenly felt the nudge of God's Spirit whispering in my ear: *Talk to them about Jesus.* Don't get me wrong: I wasn't hearing voices, but I knew that God was trying to get my attention. Then I got a case of the "yeah-buts." You know the routine . . . and the excuses: "Yeah—but Lord, I'm just here to buy some stamps," or "Yeah—but Lord, I'm not real great sharing one-on-one; I'm a lot better in front of a crowd." I finally ran out of excuses and simply said, "OK, Lord—You win. Just show me how to get the conversation started."

Just then one of the missionaries grabbed a phone card from the rack on the counter and walked back to his friend. Trying not to be too obvious that I was listening in on their conversation, I overhead them discussing the cost of buying the card and how much calling time it would give each of them. That's when I jumped in. "Hey guys, you don't wanna buy that card," I said. "It's not a very good deal." They responded, "We don't?" I went on to explain to them how I had just bought a calling card from Costco membership club, and it was a lot cheaper, with four times as many calling minutes. They thanked me, then asked my name and where I lived. I asked the same questions of them.

Bob, Jim, and I all lived within a few miles of each other in a community about ten miles away. "What are you doing all the way down here?" they asked. "I was in the area," I responded. "And this is also where my business post office box is located." Their next question was, "What kind of business do you have?" "I'm in the communication business," I replied. Then I went on to explain to them how I was involved in two radio programs and a TV show, that I wrote books, and I traveled extensively speaking to various groups of people in many parts of the world. Bob and Jim seemed curious about my "business" and especially the topics of the books. "There is a thread that winds through most of my books," I answered. "It's about how you can have a personal relationship with Jesus Christ." A soon as I said the name of Jesus, they looked like they were caught in a freeze frame. This happened each time I mentioned Jesus to Bob and Jim.

By now I realized that most everyone else in line at the post office was listening to my conversation with the two Mormon missionaries. I said to Bob, "Would you like to read one of the books I wrote called *Keeping Christ in Christmas?*" He responded with a definite "yes," and then Jim asked if I would send him a copy as well. "Sure," I said, "but you guys have to promise me that if I send you each a book, you'll read the whole thing." Bob and Jim gave me their address and promised to read my book. They also wanted to send me some information on the Mormon Church.

Unfortunately, I've had no further contact with Bob and Jim. Still, I know that if they did read my book, then at least they've heard the truth about who Jesus *really* is.

It seems as if Mormons—members of the Church of Jesus Christ of Latter-day Saints (LDS)—are everywhere. For instance, I was traveling and speaking in various parts of the Philippines and saw two of their missionaries riding bikes on a narrow road in the jungle heading toward a local temple. Another time I was on vacation in Hawaii and went to see a special show at the Polynesian Cultural Center. After a great meal and performance, including hula dancers and guys tossing lit torches in the air, the audience members were invited to another pavilion to learn more about the Church of the Latter-day Saints. Two missionaries even came knocking at my door one Easter at 8:00 at night.

Without a doubt the Mormon Church is one of the wealthiest and most influential religious groups in the United States. They place great emphasis on family and clean living and make extremely effective use of the media. Mormon television and radio outlets reach millions of people each day with clever, well-done programming.

The squeaky clean image of entertainers such as Donny and Marie Osmond has been an asset to the Mormon Church. The Church of the Latter-day Saints broadcasts TV commercials that deal with everyday issues, like parenting and satisfaction in life, rather than heavy religious content. This has enabled the Mormon Church to develop a favorable impression with the general public in America. Since its founding by Joseph Smith in 1830, the Mormon Church has gradually moved from the fringes of American religion to a more mainstream position.

Mormons have used several other strategies in past years to give the appearance of being a mainstream Christian denomination:

- Eliminating from the church the controversial doctrine of polygamy (having more than one spouse or mate at one time).
- Allowing blacks to be in the priesthood (in the past they were excluded).
- Helping out with humanitarian aid when catastrophes occur.

Mormons have been working hard to appear as legitimate as Protestants, Jews, and Catholics. Not far from where I live in southern California, a Baptist pastor and a Mormon bishop have been taking turns speaking in each other's churches in order to help break down the barriers between their two groups.

But there's a downside for Mormons if they continue being involved with Protestants, Jews, Catholics, and others. How will they maintain their historic position of being the "only true church," saying that everyone else is wrong? Supposedly founder Joseph Smith received the original authoritative "only true church" statement as part of his first vision, in which he allegedly saw and interacted with God the Father and Jesus Christ. Smith basically asked them which church he should join. Here was the answer he said he received:

> I was answered that I must join none of them, for they were all wrong; and the Personage who addressed me said that all their creeds were an abomination in his sight, that those professors were all corrupt; that: "they draw near to me with their lips, but their hearts are far from me, they teach for doctrines the commandments of men, having a form of godliness but they deny the power thereof."[1]

An attempt was made by a Mormon Church leader to explain what Joseph Smith's words really meant: "By reading the passage carefully, we find that the Lord Jesus Christ was referring only to that particular group of ministers in the Prophet Joseph Smith's community who were quarreling and arguing about what church was true."[2]

Of course this explanation raises questions. If this was really
what Jesus meant, why did Joseph Smith start the Mormon Church
when all he had to do was move to a different town and find a pastor who wasn't messed up?

The History of the Mormon Church

No doubt the Mormon Church has a fascinating history, in part
because it began in the United States. It's actually divided into two
separate groups: the Church of Jesus Christ of Latter-day Saints,
headquartered in Salt Lake City, Utah; and the Reformed Church of
Jesus Christ of Latter-day Saints, headquartered in Independence,
Missouri.

Joseph Smith Jr. (aka "The Prophet") was born December 23,
1805, in Sharon, Vermont. His father, Joseph Smith Sr., was a mystic
and spent most of his time digging for imaginary buried treasure. He
also tried to mint his own money, which caught the attention of local
authorities. His mother, Lucy, had some extreme religious views and
various superstitious beliefs as well.

Joseph Smith Jr. had the start of his "prophet's call" in 1820. He
supposedly received an incredible vision in the woods, when both
God the Father and Jesus materialized and talked to him. According
to Smith's record of this incident in his book *Pearl of Great Price,* God
and Jesus had a bad view of the Christian church and the world.
They had chosen Smith to be the one to restore true Christianity.
Apparently this encounter did not make a big impression on young
Smith at the time because he was soon back digging for treasure with
his father and brother. They were trying to find Captain Kidd's plunder using "peek stones," divining rods, and plain old digging. Young
Smith claimed to have supernatural powers that supposedly helped
him decide where to dig in these searches when he used a special
stone that he put in his hat.

At age seventeen, three years after his first heavenly vision,
Smith had another one. Only this time it was a bedside visit from the
angel Moroni, son of Mormon—the man who had the famous book
named after him. Three times Moroni repeated his commission to
the mesmerized treasure hunter. During this heavenly encounter,
Smith was also told about a book written on golden plates by former
inhabitants of the continent that would contain "the fullness of the

everlasting gospel." Eventually this would become the *Book of Mormon* (BOM).

It took several years for Smith to finally write this account down. Maybe this delay caused the confusion between what Smith wrote in an early edition of *Pearl of Great Price* and what was written in a later edition. In the earlier edition, he said the messenger's name was Moroni. Yet in a later edition, Smith—with his same "prophet" authority—named the messenger Nephi. In current editions of the book, Mormon scribes have once again named the messenger Moroni. Who was the real nighttime visitor of Smith—Moroni or Nephi?

Smith dug up the "golden plates" in 1827 in the hill Cumorah near Palmyra, New York. Smith used the "Urim and Thummim"— gigantic, miraculous glasses—to begin translating what he called the "Reformed Egyptian" hieroglyphics that were inscribed on the golden plates. It took Smith almost two years (1827–29) to translate the plates. Smith would sit behind a curtain, gazing into a hat (containing a "peep" stone) and dictating each line to a scribe on the other side of the curtain. The use of a "peep" stone to get information that is otherwise unavailable is called "scrying" (meaning "to read") and is an occult practice that is still popular today.

Early on, Smith played recklessly with the truth and had a reputation for being a fraud by those who knew him well. On March 20, 1826, a court found him guilty of money digging with a "peep" stone. In those days, people who did scrying were thought of as con men.

A schoolteacher named Oliver Cowdery visited Smith at his father-in-law's house and was converted to the "prophet's" religion. Oliver soon became one of the "scribes" who wrote down what Smith said the plates read. Neither Oliver nor anyone else but Smith actually saw the "golden plates." Joe and Oliver became good friends and on May 15, 1829, experienced an incredible supernatural event. Supposedly heaven was so excited about the translation work the two friends were doing that Peter, James, and John dispatched John the Baptist—in person, to Pennsylvania—with orders to confer the "Aaronic Priesthood" on Joe and Oliver.

This amazing event is recorded in *Pearl of Great Price,* including the account of Oliver baptizing Joe and vice versa. They also had an interesting time predicting future events "which would shortly" come to pass. (Smith was careful not to be too specific in recording the details of these future predictions because Mormon prophecies did not happen on schedule.) Joe then returned to New York and completed the translation—from "the plates"—of the *Book of Mormon*, which was then published and copyrighted in 1830. Martin Harris, a wealthy farmer who was helping Smith, mortgaged his farm to finance the publishing of the first edition of the BOM.

Before the BOM was published, Harris decided to see if the plates and translation were authentic. He took a sample to Charles Anthon, a professor at Columbia College, and reported back to Smith that the professor recognized the characters he had seen as "Egyptian, Chaldaic, Assyriac, and Arabic" and that the translation was accurate. Sometime later, Anthon heard about Harris's report to Smith and fired off a long letter to Mr. E. D. Howe, a researcher of Joseph Smith and the origins of the Mormon Church. The heart of Professor Anthon's letter to Howe was: "The whole story about my having pronounced the Mormonite inscription to be 'Reformed Egyptian hieroglyphics' is perfectly false." Anthon well remembered that the paper contained anything else but "Egyptian hieroglyphics."[3]

On April 6 of that same year, Oliver Cowdery and two others officially started a new religious society called The Church of Christ, which eventually became The Church of Jesus Christ of Latter-day Saints. The church grew rapidly, and from 1831–44, Smith set up Mormon strongholds in Illinois, Missouri, and Ohio. But no matter where they went, Mormons always attracted hostility and persecution. This happened for two main reasons: non-Mormons were suspicious of Mormon practices, or they simply didn't trust Smith.

During this same period of time, Smith continued receiving revelations on new and different doctrines, as well as advice concerning what to do next and where to go. In 1833 the *Book of Commandments* was published, containing sixty-five chapters compiling these new revelations. A second edition was released in 1835 under the new title *Doctrine and Covenants*. It was eventually considered "inspired scripture" along with the BOM.

By 1838, Smith and the Mormons had been kicked out of Missouri and into Illinois. It was here that Smith helped to develop the booming city of Nauvoo. This location is where Smith came up with new revelations about the origin and destiny of the human race, the Godhead, baptism for the dead, eternal progression, sacred temple ordinances, and polygamy (multiple marriages). Smith's poor wife Emma was threatened that she would be "destroyed" if she resisted the idea.[4]

The local newspaper, *The Nauvoo Expositor,* started publishing stories exposing the Mormon practice of polygamy, which created tremendous tensions between non-Mormons and Mormons. Because Smith was the mayor of Nauvoo, he thought he was in a major power position and ordered that the newspaper be destroyed. Non-Mormons had had enough, and Smith found himself, along with his brother Hyrum, jailed in Carthage, Illinois, awaiting trial. But Smith and Hyrum never made it to trial. On June 27, 1844, a mob of about two hundred people attacked the jail and murdered both men. This event gave the fledgling church what it needed—a martyr.

After Smith's death, there was a power struggle for church leadership. Brigham Young won and led a large number of Latter-day Saints west. In 1847 they eventually settled in the valley of the Great Salt Lake. Young made polygamy an official practice of the church and personally had twenty wives and fifty-seven children. The group of Mormons who didn't follow Young west remained in the Missouri/Illinois area and was led by Smith's wife Emma and his son Joseph III. They formed the Reorganized Church of Jesus Christ of Latter-day Saints, headquartered today in Independence, Missouri.

The Mormons stopped practicing polygamy in 1890 because of a federal law against it, which included fines and imprisonment. The fourth prophet/president, Wilford Woodruff, withdrew polygamy as a practice but not as a doctrine. He didn't have much choice because the government was threatening the very existence of all Mormon temples. Utah actually was denied statehood at least six times because of polygamy.[5]

Despite all the difficulties and troubles over polygamy, the Mormon Church became strong and successful under Brigham Young's ironfisted rule. He advocated the death penalty for any white mixing blood with a "Negro" and also taught that Jesus had been conceived through actual sexual relations between God the Father and the Virgin Mary.

What Do Mormons Believe?

Mormons are known for their thriftiness, strong emphasis on family, and missionary zeal. They require all members to give one-tenth of their income to the church, which results in a very wealthy organization. The Mormon Church also encourages what it calls "fast offerings." This involves giving up two meals on the first Sunday of each month; the amount saved is then turned over to the Church as a voluntary donation to support the poor. Mormons also strongly encourage young men at age nineteen and ladies at age twenty-one to dedicate two years of their lives to missionary work. Education also ranks very high in Mormon circles. While most of these values and ideals are commendable, they don't get to the heart of what Mormons actually believe.

In *Doctrine and Covenants,* Joseph Smith outlines the following "new revelations": plurality of gods (polytheism), God as an exalted man, three degrees of heaven, eternal progression, baptism for the dead, and multiple marriages (polygamy). There are also several prophecies of Smith's in *Doctrine and Covenants* that didn't come true (which makes Smith a false prophet according to what the Bible teaches [Deut. 18:20–22]).

Mormons believe that god—the heavenly father—is really an exalted man. He is one of a species of gods that existed before the heavenly father that currently rules the earth. Mormons believe that he's not the eternal creator; instead, they believe that he was created by another god who had been created by someone else, and so on and so on—throughout history. Because they believe in polytheism, Mormons teach that the universe is inhabited by different gods who procreate spirit children, who in turn are clothed with bodies on different planets.

Mormons teach that the father-god of our present universe was created out of eternal matter, which is full of "intelligences." He then became a spirit being, grew to maturity, and was sent to a planet (other than earth), where he lived as a man and tried to learn all that he could as he grew up. He finally died and was resurrected. He then attained godhood, so he returned to a heavenly dwelling with a new body of flesh and bones and joined with his goddess wife, known as mother-god. They started having millions of spirit children who in time populated the earth. Each of these children was originally an "intelligence" who at one time lived in eternal matter. Mormons call the spirit world domain—where all this takes place—"the preexistence."[6]

Mormons teach that when the father-god and the mother-god began having spirit children, the very first creation was Jesus Christ, followed by his brother Lucifer; then everyone else was created to populate the earth. When creation of the spirit children was completed, father-god called a meeting—the Council of Heaven—to share with everyone his plan for them. The spirit children were to live on earth where they could be tested and eventually return to him after they died. A savior was needed, and there were two possible nominees: Jesus and Lucifer.

Younger brother Lucifer (also called Satan) didn't like it when Jesus was picked, so he rebelled. He took on the armies of heaven in a great war, led by Michael the Archangel, and was badly defeated. He was then thrown down to earth—condemned to live as a spirit— never having a human body. But meanwhile, the father-god instructed Jesus to work with other spirit children to use eternal matter to create the earth, Adam and Eve, and all the animals.[7]

Some of the spirit children descendants of Adam and Eve had only fought halfheartedly in the Great War against Satan. Because of the way they fought, they were sentenced to be born mortals with black skin, as part of the ancestry of Cain. Mormon church leaders— including Joseph Smith, Brigham Young, and Bruce McConkie— have expressed racist attitudes and teachings that have never been officially rejected by the church in spite of its declaration in 1978 to allow blacks into the priesthood.

Mormons teach that when Jesus came to earth to be the savior of humanity, he was born of Mary but was not conceived by the Holy Spirit. Instead, he was conceived when the father-god came to earth and had sexual intercourse with Mary. Many Mormon leaders have believed and taught this—from Brigham Young to Ezra Taft Benson.[8]

After his death on the cross, Jesus "gained fullness" through his resurrected body. He went back to heaven, fully exalted, and now reigns with the father-god in power and glory. Joseph Smith taught that eventually Jesus would take over for the father-god when he moves on to a higher level of glory and progression.[9]

Although there is no official position on whether Jesus was married, Mormon teaching requires celestial marriage for godhood. LDS apostle Orson Pratt strongly suggests that Jesus not only married but committed polygamy as well. At the wedding at Cana, Jesus supposedly wed Mary, Martha, and the other Mary. LDS apostle Orson Hyde also taught that Jesus actually had children before he died on the cross. Mormons believe you are married for this life and eternity if you get married in the temple. By getting married in the temple, couples also get spirit-children.

Mormons believe that baptism by immersion is a requirement for salvation. Because infant baptism of any form is not accepted, after children reach the age of eight, they are baptized. The LDS church also believes in baptism for the dead. It is needed to secure the salvation of those who never had an opportunity during life to believe Mormon teaching. An individual baptized in the temple in proxy for someone who has died accomplishes baptism for the dead.

Mormons have a concept of the priesthood in which their God has placed only their church presidents, apostles, high priests, seventies, and elders. They all have specific responsibilities in the process of acting in the name of the Lord for the salvation of humanity. The Bible, however, teaches about a universal priesthood of believers. This means that each believer can come individually to God and is able to speak to other people about the work Jesus did on the cross (1 Pet. 2:9–10).

Concerning life after death, Mormons teach that those who are proven worthy will receive their own planet to inhabit. In addition, there are three degrees of heaven that you can obtain depending on your worthiness. Hell, as defined in the Bible, does not exist, but there is spirit-prison hell that is only a temporary state.

Keep in mind that there is a difference between what Mormons say and what they teach. Their "politically correct" public image simply masks their unorthodox beliefs.

The Book of Mormon *and Beyond*

The Mormons have "four standard works" of authorized scripture. They consider the first three—*Doctrine and Covenants, Pearl of Great Price,* and the initial volume of the *Book of Mormon*—to be the inspired word of God. While Mormons claim full and absolute accuracy for these three works, they have some doubts about their "fourth standard work": the King James Version of the Bible. They only accept it as "inspired" so far as it is "translated correctly." LDS apostle Orson Pratt said he doubted even one verse of the New Testament had escaped pollution or conveyed the same sense now that it did in the original manuscripts.[10] This seems contradictory considering the fact that the BOM contains approximately twenty-seven thousand words copied—often to the letter—from the King James Version of the Bible. (For example, compare 2 Nephi 12–14 to Isaiah 2–14.)

The BOM covers the history of two ancient civilizations that were located on the American continent. According to the Mormon version of history, the first of these great civilizations left the Tower of Babel about 2,250 BC, crossed over into Europe, and emigrated to the east coast of what is now Central America. This entire civilization, known as the Jaredites, was completely destroyed because of their "corruption."

The second group supposedly left Jerusalem around 600 BC, before the city was destroyed and Israel was taken captive by Babylonia. Again, according to the Mormon's version of history, this group crossed the Pacific Ocean, landing in America. This original group split into two nations, the Nephites and the Lamanites.

The author of the BOM is Mormon, the commander in chief of the Nephites. The story goes that after he completed his part of the account on gold plates, Mormon gave the plates to his son Moroni, who added a few words of his own and then hid the plates in the hill Cumorah. The account claims that Jesus visited the American continent, revealed himself to the Nephites, preached the gospel to them, and instituted the communion service and baptism. The Nephites were all killed in a battle with the Lamanites. According to Mormon history, the Lamanites were the principal ancestors of the American Indians. (Supposedly the Lamanites, because of their evil deeds, were cursed with dark skin.)

Approximately fourteen hundred years later, Joseph Smith dug up the gold plates that had been buried by Moroni and translated them into the BOM. There were reportedly four classes of plates that Smith found:

1. Plates of Nephi. These recorded mainly secular history and some sacred events.
2. Plates of Mormon. This set was a condensation of Nephi that was made by Mormon and included his commentaries as well as historical notes by his son Moroni.
3. Plates of Ether. This set was also abbreviated by Moroni and recorded the history of the Jaredites.
4. Plates of Laban or "brass plates." These supposedly came from Jerusalem and appear in the form of extracts in Nephite records. They are given over to quotations from the Hebrew Scriptures and genealogies.

According to Mormon thought, the BOM then interprets Old Testament prophecy, claims to be part of the new covenant to Israel, and supposedly is "another witness" to the truth of the Christian gospel.[11] Unfortunately, most of the time this "witness" contradicts the Bible. Also, there is other evidence, including both scientific and archaeological evidence, that does not support the BOM.

As stated earlier, Professor Charles Anthon of Columbia University could not verify that the "Reformed Egyptian hieroglyphics" were an actual language. In fact, no one has found anything remotely close to a language called "Reformed Egyptian." All highly regarded linguists who have examined the evidence supplied by the Mormons have rejected it as mythical.

Since the BOM reports the development of two great civilizations on the American continent, there should be plenty of archaeological evidence left behind to evaluate. For example, the BOM speaks of at least thirty-eight "mighty cities" built by the Nephites and Jaredites.[12] No evidence has been found to support their claims. Not only have leading archaeological researchers rejected the claims of the *Book of Mormon* as to the existence of these civilizations; researchers also have produced considerable evidence to show the impossibility of the accounts given in the Mormon Bible.[13]

Although Joseph Smith claimed that the BOM was the "most correct of any book on the earth,"[14] he still found it necessary to add thirteen key Mormon doctrines that were missing in the BOM. And just like the BOM, *Doctrine and Covenants* has been revised as new editions were published. It's also interesting to note that approximately four thousand word changes have been made in the BOM since it was first published. Yet the Bible says in 1 Peter 1:25: "but the word of the Lord endures forever."

Pearl of Great Price was translated in part from papyri fragments that Smith bought from a traveling lecturer in 1835 (along with some Egyptian mummies). Smith claimed the Egyptian hieroglyphics on the parchment were a documentation of things written by Abraham while he was in Egypt. This "Book of Abraham" was a part of *Pearl of Great Price.* More than one hundred years later these pieces of parchment finally showed up and were returned to the Mormon Church. Unfortunately, upon close examination by non-Mormon and Mormon experts, the fragments turned out to be nothing more than an Egyptian funeral manuscript giving instructions to embalmers. Yet Smith had taken parts of these Egyptian characters; created actual words, such as *water;* and developed pages of teaching on various doctrines. But once again, in spite of science contradicting Smith's writings, the *Encyclopedia of Mormonism* unblushingly states that when Smith looked at the

Egyptian hieroglyphics on the pieces of papyrus, he "sought revelation from the Lord" and "received the book of Abraham."[15]

The BOM also lacks accurate historical information. For example, glass windows, a compass, and steel were all mentioned, even though none had been invented yet. Joseph Smith obviously wasn't a very good student of history or ancient customs.

A key to understanding Mormons is recognizing that they have absolutely unshakable faith in Joseph Smith, their first prophet. Facts do not matter to them. Smith is their source of divine revelation, the foundation of their entire viewpoint.[16]

Are Mormons Christians?

While doing research for this book, I decided to check out the official Web site for the Church of Latter-day Saints. On the site was a section called "Are Mormons Christians?" Gordon B. Hinckley, president of the LDS, gave the following answer:

> We are Christians in a very real sense and that is coming to be more and more widely recognized. Once upon a time people everywhere said we are not Christians. They have come to recognize that we are, and that we have a very vital and dynamic religion based on the teachings of Jesus Christ.
>
> We, of course, accept Jesus Christ as our Leader, our King, our Savior. The dominant figure in the history of the world, the only perfect Man who ever walked the earth, the living Son of the living God. He is our Savior and our Redeemer through whose atoning sacrifice has come the opportunity of eternal life.
>
> Members of the Church of Jesus Christ of Latter-day Saints pray and worship in the name of Jesus Christ. He is the center of our faith and the head of our Church. The Book of Mormon is Another Testament of Jesus Christ and witnesses of His divinity, His life, and His Atonement.

Sounds pretty convincing. As I searched other parts of their official church Web site, I noticed similar statements and ideas. It wasn't until I started digging deeper and looking carefully at what they were actually saying that I saw a very clever deception in the claims they were making. Here's another example from the Web site that Mormons call "The Plan of Salvation." Read it carefully.

You lived with your Heavenly Father as one of His spirit

children before you began your life on Earth. You were happy there, but God knew that you could not continue to progress unless you left Him for a time.

So He presented His plan—the plan of salvation. It allowed you to come to Earth, where you would gain a physical body and would have experiences that would help you to learn and grow. The purpose of the plan is to help you become more like Him.

Heavenly Father knew that while you were on Earth you would make mistakes—everyone does. So, as part of His plan, He provided a Savior, Jesus Christ, who would make it possible for sins to be forgiven, and for all people who accept His sacrifice to return to live with Heavenly Father.

The fact that you are living on Earth means that you accepted Heavenly Father's plan and came here wanting to do all you could to receive all He has to offer.

The marvelous thing about Heavenly Father's plan is that by following it, not only can you return to Him after you die—you can also find peace and happiness in this life.

You don't have to read anymore than the first paragraph to realize something's wrong. Notice how they talk about "soul progression." We'll talk more about this later in this chapter.

The Mormons have spent the last several years trying to get their church accepted as Christian. Stephen Robinson, chairman of the Department of Ancient Scripture at Brigham Young University (a Mormon school), wrote a book called *Are Mormons Christians?* In the first chapter of his book, he gives a definition of *Christian* that is so broad that a lot of people—including Mormons—could be considered Christians. In fact, he basically uses a definition straight out of *Webster's Dictionary*.

In today's culture we must be cautious of assuming that just because someone calls Jesus Lord that he or she is Christian as the Bible defines Christian. Jesus taught that the way is narrow and that not all who call Him Lord are really Christians (Matt. 5:20; 7:13–23). If you carefully examine the facts, you realize that even though Mormons acknowledge Jesus as Lord, they have redefined *Lord* so much that the meaning is completely different. The Mormon's *Lord* Jesus had a beginning in time, was not part of the Trinity, was not conceived by the Holy Spirit, and is not the Creator-God who is holy and worthy of our worship.

As we discussed in an earlier chapter, the Bible teaches that you only have the right to be called a Christian if you receive Christ (John 1:12) and believe that He is the eternal Word who has always been with the one true God (John 1:1) and who became flesh (John 1:14). Unfortunately, the Mormons are teaching about "another Jesus" that the Bible warns about in 2 Corinthians 11:4. Are Mormons true Christians? Even though the masquerade is good, the answer is still no.

Key Differences
between the Mormon Church and Christianity

There are many significant differences between what Mormons and Christians believe. Here are some of the important ones.

- Mormons teach that God the Father is a mere man with flesh and bones. Christians believe that God the Father is spirit and does not have a body of flesh and bones (John 4:24).
- Mormons claim they have received further revelation of biblical teaching in books like *Pearl of Great Price, Doctrine and Covenants,* and the *Book of Mormon.* The Bible makes it very clear that the Bible is the final Word and warns that nothing is to be taken away or added (Rev. 22:18–19).
- Mormons believe that matter is eternal but God is not. Christians believe that God is eternal (Gen. 21:33; Deut. 33:27; Jer. 10:10).
- Mormons teach that Lucifer is the younger brother of Jesus. Christians believe that Satan is a created being (Ezek. 28:12, 14–17).
- Mormons believe that everyone who has ever lived existed first as an "intelligence" who lived in eternal matter. The Bible teaches that every person had his or her beginning on earth at the time of conception (Ps. 139:13–16).
- The Mormon concept of salvation comes in two parts: general and individual. They believe that all humanity will be saved when they are resurrected and will be judged on their works. If a person wants to earn forgiveness from personal sins, he must meet certain requirements, including faith in Christ, baptism by immersion, obedience to the teachings of

the Mormon Church, good works, and the keeping of the commandments of God. Christians believe that salvation is a free gift of God through faith not works (Rom. 6:23; 10:9; Eph. 2:8–9).

- Mormons believe that everyone must learn to become a god, the same as all gods have done, by moving from one small degree to another. The Bible is clear that there is only one God—none before and none after. He is changeless (Isa. 43:10; Hos. 11:9; Mal. 3:6).

- Mormons believe that the Trinity is three gods—with distinct bodies, except for the Holy Spirit, who has never been able to become a man and has only a spirit body. Christians believe that the Trinity is one God whose essence is found in three persons (John 1:3; Col. 1:16; 2 Cor. 5:19; Eph. 2:18; Gen. 1:26; Ps. 110:1; Isa. 7:14; 48:16; 61:1; 1 Cor. 8:6; Heb. 1:8–10; Acts 5:3–4; Deut. 6:4).

- Mormons accept as the "word of God" the *Book of Mormon, Doctrine and Covenants* and *Pearl of Great Price*; they do not, however, accept the whole Bible because of errors in translation. They also believe that God continues to speak new revelations because they are necessary. Christians believe that there is no new revelation from God and that the Bible is complete and without error (2 Tim. 3:16; Jude 3; Gal. 1:8; 2 Pet. 1:3).

- Mormons teach that most of humanity will end up in one of three levels of heaven: telestial, terrestrial, or celestial. Eternal life in celestial heaven is only for Mormons. Christians believe that heaven is God's dwelling place (Ps. 73:25) and will be the home for all those who believe in the complete payment for personal sins accomplished by Jesus on the cross (1 John 4:10). Ultimately, heaven is to be in the presence of Christ (Luke 23:43; John 14:3; 2 Cor. 5:8; 1 John 3:2).

Think about It

1. What do you think is the main thing that attracts teenagers to Mormonism? Why?

2. What is the ultimate goal of Mormonism? What about Christianity?

3. When you have the opportunity to talk with a Mormon about your relationship with Christ, remember the following things:

- Try to discover what attracted them to Mormonism. Use that as a springboard to talk about what brought you to Jesus.
- Refer to the Bible frequently and let them know that is where the support for your faith comes from. Also, share with them all the evidence for the Bible being reliable (see "The Bible" in chap. 11).
- Focus on the fact that Jesus was more than a prophet—He is God.
- Salvation is a gift from God.

Chapter Seven

The New Age Movement

A re you tired of reality? Looking for an escape from your boring, dull life? Then check this out. Maybe it's just what you've been looking for!

Get real . . . or Ridiculous

Create and customize your Sim to be just like you—or someone else. Be rich, powerful, popular, famous, or infamous.

Life is what you make of it

Let your imagination run wild. Choose your online role and play your way in this unpredictable, infinite, online world.

Speak for yourself

Meet, flirt with, and get to know other Sims through chat, instant messages, and hundreds of new expressive gestures.

Build a home and a livelihood

Build your dream home, the trendiest boutique, or the hottest neighborhood hangout around.

Be roommates and colleagues

Develop a network of friends, go into business with your housemates, or improve the neighborhood.

Welcome to the twisted-sitcom-as-computer game "The Sims." It's a virtual world built from the imaginations of thousands of people like you and me. As one Web site says, "Be somebody else with somebody else."

Using the Sims and its expansion packs, you create a simulated person or family and help them get through their daily lives as they try to decorate their homes, hold down jobs, make friends, and win the hearts of the other computer-controlled "sims" in the game. Because you control only your sims' actions and not the outcomes, the whole experience is filtered through the Sims creator Will Wright's satiric decontamination of human behavior. Try to kiss the neighbor's husband before you've wooed him sufficiently and you might get cruelly rebuffed—and your kids could be barred from visiting their playmates. Or if you become overly materialistic, your sims may end up in a house filled with old broken-down grandfather clocks and combustible stoves as you struggle to keep everything in working order.

With the Sims—the best-selling PC game ever that exploded with its online version—you can live a parallel life or a life partially online, which has become second nature to anyone under twenty-five. Virtual reality-type online games have become huge outlets for competition as well as forums for social interaction. Industry experts say even shoot-'em-up action games can be beneficial socially. The most widely played online action game is "Counter-Strike," where you play on one of two teams—Terrorists or Counter-Terrorists—in a variety of scenarios, including rescuing hostages and planting or defusing bombs. It's estimated that every night, without fail, there are 100,000 or more people online playing Counter-Strike.

Playing make-believe war games, role playing games, or even setting up a parallel life online can be challenging, fun, and entertaining. But it's not real. There are people today, however, who honestly believe they can change reality into any form they want. They believe that "reality is what you make it," and they are part of the New Age movement.

What Is the New Age Movement?

Time magazine calls the New Age "a combination of spirituality and superstition, fad and force, about which the only thing certain is that it is not new."[1] Essentially, New Age is nothing but ancient Hinduism and occultism repackaged. Leaders within the movement say it is amazing what you can get people to do when you take away the Hindu and occultic terminology and use twenty-first-century language.

New Age can be defined as the growing penetration of Eastern and occultic mysticism into Western culture. The term *New Age* refers to the Aquarian Age, which some New Agers believe is dawning, bringing with it an era of enlightenment, peace, prosperity, and perfection. Of course, that's exactly what Satan would like us to think!

In reality, the New Age movement is simply opening the doors, even wider than before, to his destructive influence in our culture.

New Age is another weapon in the devil's arsenal to lure us from God's truth. The following statistics give a brief glimpse of the progress Satan is making in shaping Americans' thinking, especially in the past ten years.

- 45 percent believe in psychic or spiritual healing—the power of the human mind to heal the body
- 50 percent believe in ESP, or extrasensory perception
- 42 percent believe that houses can be haunted
- 41 percent believe that people on earth are sometimes possessed by the devil
- 38 percent believe that ghosts, spirits of dead people, can come back in certain places and situations
- 36 percent believe in telepathy—communication between minds without using the traditional five senses
- 33 percent believe that extraterrestrial beings have visited earth at some time in the past
- 32 percent believe in clairvoyance—the power of the mind to know the past and predict the future
- 28 percent believe that people can hear from or communicate mentally with someone who has died
- 28 percent believe in astrology—that the position of the stars and planets can affect people's lives
- 26 percent believe in witches
- 25 percent believe in reincarnation, that is, the rebirth of the soul in a new body after death
- 15 percent believe in channeling, or allowing a "spirit-being" to temporarily assume control of a human body during a trance[2]

It's amazing how popular New Age has become. Most bookstores offer a massive selection of books relating to various aspects of New Age, and entire magazines are devoted to the movement. New Age concepts have also been steadily introduced and made popular by a number of celebrities, such as actress Shirley MacLaine or John Edward, best-selling author and host of the TV show *Crossing Over.* John—a psychic medium, author, and lecturer—claims to have helped thousands throughout the last fifteen years with his ability to predict future events and communicate with those who have "crossed over" to the "other side."

Then there is New Age guru and best-selling author Deepak Chopra. *Time* magazine calls him the "poet-prophet of alternative medicine." The lobby of Chopra's two-story training center has shelves of Hindu statutes, bottles of massage oil, and "Eternal Om" CDs. In his book *Golf for Enlightenment,* Chopra shares spiritual tips for improving your game, including "Be one with the ball." He believes people can become one with anything: "If you're in unity consciousness, the whole world is animated to you. You can talk to trees and stars. Everything is part of your body."[3]

New Age and occultic themes are also found in movies and TV series, including the *Star Wars* saga and the *Star Trek* series. New Age products and gadgets flood the marketplace: singing Tibetan bowls, crystals, pyramids, tarot cards, charms, fortune-telling devices, computer software, and even "rebirthing" tanks.

The New Age movement has become more than a fad; for many, it's a lifestyle. From the outside, the New Age movement may seem appealing. It even appears to have some good intentions: to take care of the homeless, to eliminate disease and racial tension, and to protect the environment. That sounds good—but what beliefs fuel the New Age movement?

Foundational Beliefs of the New Age Movement

The following six principles of New Age thinking form the "revolutionary understanding" shared by those involved in the movement. As you will see, each is a clever, subtle counterfeit of biblical Christianity.

1. All Is One/One Is All (Monism)

According to New Agers, every particle in the universe is interconnected. Everything swims in this huge cosmic interconnected ocean. There is no difference between rocks, trees, humans, animals, and God. We are all the same. The reason we have problems in our world today is not because of evil but ignorance. We are ignorant of the fact that we are all interconnected.

2. God Is Everything/Everything Is God (Pantheism)

New Agers say that everything in creation is part of God—trees, snails, people, and so forth. Everything has a divine (godlike) nature. They say the idea of a personal God needs to be abandoned. You don't need a savior because you are part of God. If a god (he or she) does exist at all, "it" really just started a "big bang" many years ago and is now only an impersonal force floating around in the cosmos somewhere.

What are the implications? It allows the Wiccan religion to worship the creation—"mother earth" (rocks, sun, moon, etc.)—rather than the Creator (God). New Agers say that since we are all gods, we might as well get good at it. (Sounds a bit like Genesis 3:5 when Satan deceitfully tells Adam and Eve that if they eat the fruit of a particular tree they will be like God.)

New Agers have actually reduced God to the human level so He is no different from you and me.

3. You Are a Little God (Self-Realization)

New Agers believe that because we are all gods we must become "cosmically conscious" of our godhood. They say that is what Jesus did. He was nothing more than an enlightened master, like a character out of a *Star Wars* movie. He was a dynamic teacher and an incredible person because he came to grips with the fact that he was a little god. So like Jesus, everyone else must come to realize that they are gods, too, and start living accordingly.

New Agers say, "We, too, share in the Christ-consciousness within us. The savior in us is replacing the Savior out there. There is no need for a Christ because we can save ourselves."

New Agers teach that reincarnation makes all this possible. The birth, death, and rebirth process we go through over hundreds and even thousands of years helps us get in touch with our karma. The object is to keep correcting our mistakes through the various lifetimes until we reach a point of perfection and become a god.

4. A New World Order

New Agers believe the countries of the world are coming together and eventually national boundaries will be unnecessary. People are all working to reach an omega point—ultimate peace. Yet it will only happen when we have a one-world government and a one-world religion.

Because of the unsettling world situation today, people are primed for someone to emerge as a leader, someone who has the answer for all our problems, someone to lead the entire world. Ten nations in Europe are testing the idea of using one currency. Countries that were once divided are united again. New Agers see all this as ushering in a New World Order—a counterfeit for the kingdom of God.

5. Reality Is What You Make It (Relative Truth)

New Agers say reality is determined by what you believe, which is essentially the premise of virtual reality. If you change what you believe, you can change reality. Because reality is what you make it, there are no such things as moral absolutes or good and evil. Reality is what you think is good, even if someone else thinks it is evil.

A TV talk show host was interviewing the head of a militant homosexual organization. This leader was pushing for their members to start having sex with young children under the age of five. The reporter was outraged and said so. The guest replied with, "Hey lady, that is my truth. And even though it isn't your truth, it doesn't matter what you think."

What about premarital sex? It's OK if you think it's OK—just use a condom. Without moral absolutes, all sex is good sex—between adults and children, or even between people and animals—as long as you think it is good.

The world is now a huge potpourri of "anything goes." Everyone is developing their own ethics and codes of conduct, and the result is total confusion, total chaos. Research points out that the younger a person is, the more susceptible he or she is to believing that truth is relative.[4]

6. A New Way of Thinking (Holistic Thinking)

New Agers believe we need to develop a new way of thinking about old problems—a "paradigm shift." We need to think "holistically." If we are all interconnected particles in this cosmic ocean, and if we all are part of God, then we are able to think on one level. This new way of thinking only comes from a "mystical spiritual awakening"—by getting in touch with our inner child.

Key Differences
between the New Age Movement and Christianity

There are significant differences between what New Age followers and Christians believe. Here are some of the important ones.

- New Agers believe that "all is one and one is all," that all matter is interconnected. The Bible teaches something entirely different: "because by Him everything was created, in heaven and on earth, the visible and the invisible, whether thrones or dominions or rulers or authorities—all things have been created through Him and for Him. He is before all things, and by Him all things hold together" (Col. 1:16–17). God is separate from His creation. The Bible also tells us that we are separated from God because of our sin (Rom. 3:23). In New Age teaching there is no need for forgiveness because we are all one vast interconnected ocean.

- New Agers believe that "God is everything and everything is God." Christians believe that God is a person not an impersonal force. God is not an "it" or a "force." He is alive, and He is our personal Lord and Savior. The Bible is filled with His attributes, and they tell us what a great and awesome God He really is (Deut. 6:4; Eph. 1:3).

- New Agers believe that Jesus was nothing more than an enlightened master who came to understand that He was a "little god." Christians believe that Jesus was fully God and fully man. They believe that Jesus is the Creator and the Sustainer, who had no beginning and has no end (John 1:1; 8:57–58; 10:30; Titus 2:13; Heb. 2:16–18; Matt. 1:18; 4:2; Col. 2:9).

- New Agers believe that since we are all "little gods," we must become "cosmically conscious" of the fact that we are gods. Christians believe that we are not gods, though we are created in God's image. He is the great and awesome God. The Bible teaches that we are to have no other gods before Him—including ourselves. Satan learned the hard way about trying to become his own god. That's the desire that got him kicked out of heaven in the first place (Gen. 1:26; Exod. 20:3; Ps. 77:3; Isa. 14:12–14).

- New Agers believe that there's no need for a savior because, as little gods, we can save ourselves. Christians believe we can't save ourselves, that salvation is a free gift from God. Jesus died on the cross to take the punishment for our sin so we could experience a new life and forgiveness for our sins. There is no second chance to come back and fix our mistakes. The Bible is clear when it says we die only once and then we are judged (Rom. 5:8; 6:23; Eph. 2:8–9; Heb. 9:27).

- New Agers believe the countries of the world are coming together. Christians believe that only God will create a new heaven and earth. There will not be harmony or peace in this world until Jesus—the Prince of Peace—comes to live in the hearts of people (Isa. 65:17; 9:6; 2 Thess. 3:16).

- New Agers believe that reality is determined by what we believe and truth is relative. Christians believe that God has placed the sense of good and evil in our hearts and that truth is absolute (John 8:32; 14:6; Rom. 2:15).

- New Agers believe that human nature is neither good nor bad but open to constant transformation. Christians believe that all of humanity is born in sin and each person is guilty before a holy God (Rom. 3:9–11, 23).

- New Agers believe we must get in touch with our inner child in order to develop a new way of thinking about old problems. Christians believe that we change the way we think by renewing our minds. We are capable of thinking only in human terms, but God enables us to have an eternal perspective as a result of being new creations in Christ. The way to fully develop this new way of thinking is to allow God to readjust our minds, and this only happens through the study and knowledge of His Word (Rom. 12:2; 2 Cor. 5:17).

- New Agers believe that revelation comes from a variety of sources. Christians believe that the Bible—God's inspired Word—is the only source of revelation (2 Tim. 3:16–17; Jude 3).

The New Age is probably the most widespread and powerful phenomenon affecting our culture today. Its philosophy influences music, sports, literature—in fact, nothing seems exempt, not even some churches. In dealing with the New Age movement we are really dealing with spiritual warfare against the forces of darkness, and the major battlefield is being fought in our minds.

There are many dangers associated with New Age, but the biggest danger of all is that it keeps people who are searching for spiritual truth from finding a personal relationship with Jesus Christ.

Watch for the trap of New Age thinking. Stay informed as to what is out there, and avoid deception by staying close to the Lord, and being grounded in His Word. Be on the alert for subtle influences of New Age teaching that try to creep into your mind and influence your thinking.

Think about It

1. Beside each of the six principles of New Age thinking, identify at least one example in our culture where you can see this influence. Be specific.
- All is one/one is all.
- God is everything/everything is God.
- You are a little god.
- A new world order.
- Reality is what you make it.
- A new way of thinking.

2. Read 1 Timothy 4:1–2. How do these verses relate to the New Age movement? Be specific.

3. New Agers are generally active in addressing the problems in the world. As Christians, we should be even more active in making a difference. What one thing can you do this week to help deal with a problem in your sphere of influence?

4. Why is it wrong for a Christian to believe in reincarnation? Find at least one verse in the Bible to support your answer.

Chapter Eight

Wicca and Witchcraft

You never know what you're going to hear when you eat at a McDonald's restaurant. I was meeting with a friend at a local Golden Arches when I overheard some teenagers talking about religions. One of the guys said, "What's up with Wicca? Is it just like other religions?" The girl sitting next to him in the booth responded, "You know—it's like being a Baptist or a Catholic. They're basically all the same."

Unfortunately, her response was a clear reflection of the misconceptions and confusion about faith and spirituality so many teenagers have today. If we compare the basic beliefs of Christianity and Wicca, we see how different they really are. Since both can't be right, ultimately we must decide what we believe and whom we will follow when it comes to spirituality and faith. So, let's ask the question again: What's up with Wicca?

Wicca is the fastest growing religion among high school and college students today. Teens and adults are turning to Wicca—also known as witchcraft, or the "Craft"—because this religion appears powerful, glamorous, and definitely not the norm. It is protected by law in the United States as a legitimate religion and is even practiced in some branches of the military. Pop culture today is filled with examples of Wicca and witchcraft. *Sabrina, the Teenage Witch* is a TV show about a witch and her family. *The Craft* is a movie about witchcraft. The WB network has numerous Wiccan shows, including *Buffy, the Vampire Slayer* and *Charmed*. Numerous books—including *Simple Wicca* by Michele Morgan, *Teen Witch* by Silver Ravenwolf, *The Teen Spell Book* by Jamie Wood, and the *Harry Potter* series by J. K. Rowling—and Web sites encourage teenagers to explore the world of Wicca.

Many kids (and adults)—even some who attend church—are

turning to Wicca or witchcraft for power. That's the big draw of the Craft—power to get what you want. Let's face it, life's not easy in the twenty-first century. School isn't relevant, and families don't seem to work anymore. Friends are flaky and irresponsible. The environment is a mess, the opposite sex has unrealistic expectations, armed guards patrol on campus, terrorism threatens, and a balanced life seems impossible to achieve. We need power—and lots of it—to survive.

What Is the Background of Wicca?

There is little agreement as to the roots of Wicca (an early Anglo-Saxon word for "witchcraft"). Some say it is a direct "religious" descendant of the ancient Druids and Celts. Others claim it is more modern—emerging within the past fifty to sixty years. Starhawk, author of the book *Spiral Dance: A Rebirth of the Ancient Religion of the Goddess,* thinks witchcraft had its beginnings thirty-five thousand years ago.

Basically, Wicca is part of the neo-pagan movement, attempting to revive the gods and goddesses and nature religions of ancient cultures. Wiccan and other neo-pagan groups draw from many sources—Gnosticism, occult writings, Freemasonry, Native American religions, shamanism, spiritism, and even science fiction.[1]

Some people see Wicca and Satanism as being the same thing; however, they really are very different. Wiccans today see their religion, with its origins in ancient occult religions like Druidism, as an acceptable worldview by itself. Wiccans view Satanism as a distortion of the relatively "young" Christian religion.

The rise in modern witchcraft can be traced back to the second half of the twentieth century, when a revival of pre-Christian paganism occurred in the United States and Europe. The writings of English archaeologist Gerald Gardner—including the novel *High Magic's Aid* (1949) and the book *Witchcraft Today* (1954), in which he claimed to be a witch initiated by a surviving coven—imparted much of the alleged lore and rituals of English witches. After studying occult practices in southeast Asia, he combined his Asian occult experiences with Western magical texts and developed a new religion, with worship of Mother Earth Goddess as its focus.[2] Although his claims have been questioned, covens of modern witches sprang up under Gardner's inspiration and spread to the United States in the 1960s. This form of witchcraft consists of feelings for nature, colorful rituals, and a challenge of conventional religion and society.

What Do Wiccans Believe?

There is much diversity among Wiccans. In general, Wicca is a nature religion, grounded in the worship of planet Earth, which is seen as a manifestation of the goddess, or "Great Mother." In many ways, Wicca is similar to the nature religions mentioned in the Bible, such as the fertility religions of Canaan (1 Kings 14:22–24).[3]

Most Wiccans refuse to have any centralized authority, and they are against any formal belief system. Most Wiccans build their own religion by mixing and matching various traditions and practices. Some of the better known traditions followed by witches today, besides Gardnerian, are British Traditional, Celtic, Dianic, Eclectic, Faerie, Pictish, and Strega. Like other neo-pagan religions, Wicca draws heavily on experience, so truth is relative. They're convinced that the only way to know truth is through a kind of sixth sense, or feelings.

One fundamental ethical standard taught by Wiccans is the Wiccan Rede. It states: "Do what thou will, but harm none." It's important for Wiccans to "follow their conscience."[4] They also believe in the "Rule of Three," which states that the energy from everything you do comes back to you three times as strong as you sent it out. If you cast a spell against someone, it will come back to you with three times the power.

A basic sacred text for many witches is what they call a "Book of Shadows." This is their own spiritual diary that contains spells, spiritual thoughts, and experiences. Sometimes covens keep a Book of Shadows for the entire coven.

Animism—the concept that the entire earth is a living organism—is a widespread belief in neo-pagan religions. The word *animism* means "soul" or "breath." Some witches even view animism as the heart and soul of ancient witchcraft. Some Wiccans believe that all matter, including rocks, are alive and that all objects in the universe have some kind of inner consciousness.

Some Wiccans also believe in reincarnation and something they call "Summerland." This is basically a holding place you go to after you die to wait for a new physical form. They do not believe in hell and believe that heaven is here on earth.

Wiccans do not believe that the human mind is capable of what Christians call "God." To them it is pointless to even try to understand this concept. Instead, witches believe in a god that is both masculine and feminine—a god and goddess.

What Is a Witch?

Witches are not green or covered with warts. Most of the time you can't even tell a witch simply by appearances. It's the way they live and look at life that's definitely outside of the norm.

A Wiccan witch is taught to look at the world and deal with life in a different way. At the root of the word *Wicca* is the word *wic,* which means to "bend" or "shape." Witches proport to bend and shape the laws and energies of nature, through ritual and spell casting, to produce results in the physical world. Also called magic, it is the lifeblood of witchcraft. They believe that this focused use of language, will, action, and emotion, as well as the shifting of consciousness, will achieve spiritual communion and change in the physical world.

Those involved in Wicca claim to have a depth of power far greater than is apparent to the average person. This power is drawn from several sources: spirit (God according to their definition), the elements, the ancestors, and angels. Witches use their own power—the power of the mind—to manifest what they need. They believe that over the centuries humans have suppressed many of their innate talents, including the power of the mind. We have become lazy and access only what we think we need, leaving a huge portion of our mind power unused. It is from this unused mind that abilities such as clairvoyance, telekinesis, and extrasensory perception (ESP) are found. According to those involved in Wicca, everyone has these abilities, but most people don't use them—in some cases because of fear. Witches and other enlightened souls, however, strive to strengthen these natural gifts.

God, however, reminds us in John 15:5 that we have no power on our own to achieve anything. Yet in Philippians 4:13 we have the promise that we are "able to do all things through Him who strengthens" us. Our power comes from the living God.

Unfortunately, those who practice Wicca have bought the lie that started at the beginning of human history—that we could be the masters of our own world and live independent of God. The source of that lie is the devil himself. And even though most Wiccans would say that they don't believe in Satan or the devil, that still doesn't change the reality of what has happened.

Witches celebrate eight main holidays or "sabbats." They are all centered on the solar cycles:

Greater Sabbats
1. Samhain or Halloween: October 31
2. Beltane or Rudemas: May Eve (1)
3. Imbolic or Candlemas: February 1
4. Lughnassadh or Lammas: July 31

Lesser Sabbats (note: dates vary each year)
5. Winter Solstice or Yule: December 21
6. Spring Equinox or Vernal Equinox: March 21
7. Summer Solstice or Midsummer Eve: June 21
8. Fall Equinox or Mabon: September 21

"Esbats" are the regular coven meetings that witches have and are often held during a new moon or full moon. Activities include practice of rituals, training and teaching in divination and magic (witchcraft), and initiating new members. Oftentimes witches practice going into a trance, where he or she believes the goddess possesses them. They call this process "drawing down on the sun" or "drawing down on the moon."

Many witches are also involved in spiritism—interaction with spirits, divination, magic, sorcery, and the use of psychic abilities.[5]

Wiccans say they don't believe in Satan, let alone draw power from him. The power they seek comes from a "divine entity" some recognize as "God," "Allah," "Jesus," "Mohammed," "Buddha," or whatever they choose to call it. They make no mention of Satan. Wiccans say the divine being is everything—people, plants, the earth, animals, the stars—and it's unlimited.

Wiccans often say that Satan, or the devil, is only something that Christians made up. When we study the history of religion, we will find the concept of Satan in many ancient belief systems. Take Manichaeism for example. It was an ancient religion started by a Persian sage named Mani (216–76?). Part of the doctrine of Manichaeism includes a dualistic division of the universe into opposing realms of good and evil. The Light (Spirit) lead by God and the Darkness (matter) was led by Satan. The same type of tradition can be found in other religions, such as Zoroastrianism, Judaism, and even Islam. However, there is a distinction to be made between other religious views of Satan and Christianity. In religions with dualism, the devil and God are equals; in Christianity they are not. The Bible teaches that Satan is a created being—a fallen angel—who is limited in his abilities and power while God is all-powerful, without any limitations. The Bible is very clear that Satan not only exists, but that he is also more than just an impersonal "force." You can say that you don't believe in the devil, but that doesn't really change the reality of his existence.

When it comes to obtaining power from a divine entity that people choose to call by different names, it's important to remember a foundational truth: Is the divine entity alive or dead? We can visit the tombs of Buddha, Confucius, or even Mohammed and find that they are occupied. The tomb of Jesus is empty. There is more historical evidence for the resurrection of Jesus Christ than there is for the fact that Napoleon was defeated at the Battle of Waterloo or that Julius Caesar was a Roman emperor.

The Bible makes it very clear that God is separate from His creation. In Colossians 1:16–17 we read: "because by Him everything was created, in heaven and on earth, the visible and the invisible, whether thrones or dominions or rulers or authorities—all things have been created through Him and for Him. He is before all things, and by Him all things hold together." So when Christians ask for help, they are going to the God of the universe. When Wiccans ask for help, they are looking to themselves and part of the creation rather than the Creator Himself.

Wiccan Practices

One goal of those involved in witchcraft is to exert power. They use various methods in their efforts to obtain their goal.

The Cone of Power

Wiccans utilize something called the "cone of power." This is a method of directing the energy of an individual or group for a singular purpose or to provide a connection to spirit. This "energy" is a combination of love, creativity, and spirit; and it forms the basis for a witch's power, which he or she uses to accomplish a desire. A witch builds up energy by chanting and swaying. Once the heat from the energy has reached a certain level, it must be directed into a magical tool or object where it can be held. At the desired time, the energy can be sent out to achieve the desired result.

Spell Casting

Spell casting is another practice of Wiccans. It is a form of visualization also known as "guided imagery" or "mind over matter."

The *Teen Spell* book says that spells and tools of the Craft are only as powerful as the emotions they raise inside of you. For example, if you believe that the color blue means "courage," then it will call forth that ability. Spells are primarily used to discipline the mind to create the fulfillment of our wishes. The book goes on to say that because we are so powerful we must be very careful before we direct our intent or focus on anything.

Spell casting also involves a number of ritual steps. You start by casting a circle, then purifying and cleansing yourself and any other participants. Following this you must ask for protection from the four directions and your guides, give an offering to the god and goddess, and set up the cone of power. Sounds pretty complicated doesn't it— and I've only listed part of the steps involved in spell casting.

God strictly warns us to stay away from casting spells. Check out what He says in Deuteronomy 18:10–11: "No one among you is to make his son or daughter pass through the fire, practice divination, tell fortunes, interpret omens, practice sorcery, cast spells, consult a medium or a familiar spirit, or inquire of the dead."

When we step back and look at the big picture, we realize that the power Wicca offers is quite self-centered, self-dependent, and limited. In reality, the power for living that we need in the midst of all our human weakness must come from outside ourselves. And it must be unlimited or it is of no value to us. However, this kind of power can only be found in one place.

It's described in a book and is available to all who desire it. This power is unlimited and can overcome even the most seemingly insurmountable problems. The source of this power is the living God—the God of the Bible. God is all-powerful, and His infinite power is demonstrated in many ways. He is the one who formed the unborn child in his mother's womb (Ps. 139:13–16) and created the heavens (Jer. 32:17). Nothing is too hard for Him, and He does as He pleases (Ps. 115:3). In biblical times God's power over nature was frequently demonstrated in miracles: everything from the plagues in Egypt (Exod. 7–10) to stilling a storm (Mark 4:35–41) and walking on water (Matt. 14:22–33). God's power is also obvious in His control of the course of history. In Acts 17:26 we read: "From one man He has made every nation of men to live all over the earth and has determined their appointed times and the boundaries of where they live."

One of the most amazing demonstration's of God's power is in human life and personality. In many ways, changing human personality is far more difficult than creating or lifting a large rock. It's not easy altering human nature. Yet in respect to power for this life and securing our eternal destiny, Jesus said, "With men this is impossible, but with God all things are possible" (Matt. 19:26).

Yet, by far the greatest display of God's power was the resurrection of Jesus Christ from the dead. The Bible speaks of this power in 2 Corinthians 13:4: "In fact, He was crucified in weakness, but He lives by God's power. For we also are weak in Him, yet toward you we will live with Him by God's power." This same power that brought Jesus back from the dead is available to help us live life for today and give us hope for tomorrow.

The power that Wicca offers is limited and bogus. Keep in mind that Wicca is a man-made religion of preferences that had its modern beginnings in Great Britain in the 1950s. Part of Satan's plan is to deceive us and counterfeit all that God is and does. Satan loves to disguise himself as an angel of light (2 Cor. 11:14). Because he is a created being (Ezek. 28:13, 15), his power is limited. Satan and his demonic servants work at deceiving us by appearing good and attractive. Many unsuspecting kids and adults looking for power are following sincerely deceived religious-sounding people into Satan's snare of Wicca.

Think of the search for power in another way. If you really want the kind of power that can change your life and help you face the pressures of living in the twenty-first century, why would you want to rely on another created being with limited power or on yourself trying to use a cone of power? The wise thing to do would be to find the source of unlimited power and plug into it. When you decide to follow Jesus and establish a personal relationship with Him, you tap into all the power of the universe. The search for power begins and ends with Jesus. Rely on Him to give you the strength to overcome any struggle you may be facing today. Let the promise found in Philippians 4:13 encourage and guide you: "I am able to do all things through Him who strengthens me."

Goddesses and Gods

Part of the diverseness of Wicca is the freedom to choose whom you worship. Choosing a deity is part of the appeal of Wicca. Naming a god is about what "works for you" spiritually. Some have compared the idea of Wiccan deities to a family tree, with the "All," or universal energy, at the top. The Lord and the Lady (god and goddess) are the next in line symbolizing the perfectly balanced male and female aspects of divinity that is vital to the Wiccan belief system. Finally, closest to humans on earth, are the gods and goddesses. And like you might choose a friend based on things that you were drawn to instinctively or emotionally, so you can also choose your favorite traits for a god and goddess.

There is no doctrine that dictates who or what the god and goddess must be; rather, there are ancient and symbolic descriptions of their essences and energies. The rest is left up to you to design. You can have a god who is tough or tender; fair skinned or dark; long hair or short—you can give them whatever physical form you choose.

But, it doesn't stop here. There are also additional gods and goddesses that belong to a specific "pantheon" or group of deities that serve a particular people or culture, that you can also add to your belief system. Some of the more common goddesses in Wicca are: Aphrodite, Aradia, Bast, and Demeter. A few of the more common gods are: Cernunnos, Horus, Mithra, and Taleisin.

Let's think logically for a minute. Why would you want to worship a god that you created? That "god" would obviously be no greater or no more powerful than you, so of what help could he possibly be? The God of the Bible is sovereign—supreme, free from external control. He is all-powerful (Ps. 139:13–16; Jer. 32:17; Ps. 115:3). Nothing is too hard for Him. God has the power and ability to see us through any situation in life. The ability to "create" your own deity may sound cool and fascinating, but in the end it's useless and dangerous to your soul.

Witchcraft Vs. Christian Worship

Wiccans would say that if a Christian asked God for help to cure her cancer-stricken mother, she would have to focus her mind to attain this end. "You want it with your whole body and soul because you love her and want her to be well." So what is so wrong with that? To them, using prayer is no different than using a cone of power.

The truth is, Wiccan practice is very different from prayer. The object of spell casting and the cone of power is self and exercising "inner power." The object of prayer, on the other hand, is God. Although less complex than Wiccan practices, it is supernaturally more powerful. It's much more than self-stimulation. Prayer is not a method of creating a positive mental attitude in ourselves so that we are able to do what we have asked to do. Instead, prayer is, in a big part, a matter of creating in us a right attitude with respect to God's will. Prayer is not getting God to do our will, but it's demonstrating that we are as concerned as God is that His will be done in our lives. Genuine Christians can pray confidently, knowing that our wise and good God will not always give us what we ask for but what is best for us. Psalm 84:11 says, "He does not withhold the good from those who live with integrity."

Some Wiccans say they pray to the same deity as Christians; they only use a different name. That may sound nice and politically correct—but it's not true. Wiccans and Christians do not pray to the same deity. There is a much greater distinction than only using different names. The God of the Bible is spirit (not a spirit) who does not have physical form. He cannot be limited and is the source of all life. The many references in the Bible to God's physical features are figurative language giving Him human characteristics in an attempt to make Him more understandable. The Christian God is also independent and existent in Himself (Dan. 5:23; Acts 17:28).

What God Thinks about Witchcraft

It's actually pretty easy to find out what God thinks about Wicca and witchcraft—just read the Bible! Here are a few of the verses that refer to witchcraft and reflect how God feels about it.

- 2 Chronicles 33:6: Manasseh "passed his sons through the fire in the Valley of Hinnom. He practiced witchcraft, divination, and sorcery, and consulted mediums and spiritists. He did a great deal of evil in the LORD's sight, provoking Him."
- Micah 5:12: "I will remove sorceries from your hands, and you will not have any more fortune-tellers."
- Galatians 5:19–21: "Now the works of the flesh are obvious: sexual immorality, moral impurity, promiscuity, idolatry, sorcery, hatreds, strife, jealousy, outbursts of anger, selfish ambitions, dissensions, factions, envy, drunkenness, carousing, and anything similar, about which I tell you in advance—as I told you before—that those who practice such things will not inherit the kingdom of God."

Keep in mind that while God hates witchcraft, He still loves the person who practices it. In fact, He demonstrated His love for them (and each one of us!) by allowing Jesus to die on the cross and take the punishment for their sin (Rom. 5:8).

Wicca is very real and has become a huge issue even among Christian teens. A big part of Wicca's appeal is found in being able to customize your own religious beliefs and practices. There's no personal God to serve or obey. But that also means there's no personal God to love, protect, and provide for you as well.

We need to carefully rethink our attitude toward Wicca, what the Bible teaches, and our relationship with God. Wicca is not something that we can remain neutral about, saying it's neither good nor bad. It's leading a lot of teens—even those who attend church—down an empty and deceptive path.

It's not wrong to want to have power in your life, to belong and to be loved. Wicca is very appealing to teens struggling with stress and pressures of adolescence. But the power to change your life and deal with pain, rejection, and hopelessness isn't found in casting spells, divination, or sorcery. It can only be found in a personal relationship with God through His Son Jesus Christ.

Be Cautious of the Tolerance Trap

I meet a lot of well-meaning teens who believe they have a healthy relationship with God and accept His Word—most of the time. For example, Bob doesn't think there is anything wrong with Wicca and sees it as a peaceful religion based on worshipping the earth. He says, "Wiccans do not believe in sacrificing animals or hexing people. All witches who correctly follow Wicca believe in the threefold law, which means that any spell that you cast that could have any harmful effects on a living thing will rebound upon you three times. Wicca accepts your religion so why can't you find it in your oh-so-pious-and-forgiving hearts to accept them?"

Tolerance is highly regarded by those who practice Wicca. They hold much hostility toward Christianity for making exclusive claims to being the "only way to God." But God does not offer His followers the same opportunity that Wiccans have to pick and choose what they will believe. Even if we disagree or don't understand what the Bible is teaching, God asks us to trust Him. His Word—the Bible—is without error in the original writings. It has been verified and proven more than any other book in history. When it comes to witchcraft, the Bible is very clear about how God feels. He strictly forbids practicing witchcraft or casting spells (Deut. 18:10; 2 Chron. 33:6; Mic. 5:12; Gal. 5:20). He is a holy God, and these kinds of practices are evil. It's not because God doesn't want us to enjoy life or find answers to various problems and struggles that we face. The bottom line is that He wants us to rely on Him for everything. The Lord is desperately in love with us and wants the very best for us. And because He created us, He knows what is going to make us the most fulfilled and satisfied.

It's about Truth and a Relationship

Truth becomes the ultimate foundational issue. It's not about good people or bad people—or even the freedom to choose—rather, it's where truth is to be found. Respect and independence are important but not at the risk of your eternal destiny. We have all been given a free will and can choose which path of life we will follow. However, there are consequences for the choices we make, and when it comes to religion or spirituality, it can affect our soul and eternal destiny.

Freedom is an important issue for most of us. The Bible, in fact, contains a very interesting concept concerning freedom in John 8:32. It says that when we know the truth the truth will set us free. The truth is, we all need a cure for our spiritual terminal disease called sin. Jesus died on a cross to pay the penalty for our sin and set us free to be the people that we were created to be. He is our remedy.

It's been said that you can be wrong about a lot of things in life, but you better not be wrong about God. When it comes to issues about eternity—as well as the quality of life on this planet—we need to get all the facts so we can make the wisest decision possible. But in order to get the answers we need for faith and spirituality, we need to look outside ourselves and toward the Creator of life.

As Christians, we should not discriminate against someone because she follows an alternative religion. There are a lot of good people who are sincerely wrong in what they have chosen to believe when it comes to spiritual matters. Instead, we should try to point them to the truth of who Jesus Christ is and what He has done for each one of us.

Christianity is not about a set of ideas that we buy into; it's about a relationship with a person—Jesus Christ. Throughout history, Christianity has stood up to any and all tests regarding its uniqueness and reliability. All other religions—including Wicca—tell us what we need to do. Christianity tells us what God has already done for us.

Key Differences
between Wicca, Witchcraft, and Christianity

There are significant differences between what Wiccans—those involved in witchcraft—and Christians believe. Here are some of the important ones.

- Most Wiccans believe in some form of reincarnation.[6] For witches, reincarnation is different from what a Buddhist or Hindu believes. Instead of endless "karma," witches view reincarnation as something positive that takes the soul upward in its advancement toward godhood.[7] Christians do not believe there are additional chances to come back and keep advancing our soul to new levels. The Bible is very clear when it says we die only once and then we are judged (Heb. 9:26–28; 2 Pet. 2:9).

- Wiccans believe they can influence reality through invoking invisible spirits and powers. They believe that magic is the craft of witchcraft.[8] Using magic, witchcraft, or invisible spirits is detestable to God and something He will not tolerate (Deut. 18:9–13; Isa. 8:19).

- The Wiccan view of salvation can be summed up with this statement: "We can open new eyes and see that there is nothing to be saved from; no struggle of life against the universe, no God outside the world to be feared and obeyed."[9] Christians believe that we are all born with a spiritual terminal disease called sin that causes us to disobey God and go our own willful way. This causes us to be separated from God. The remedy was Christ's death on the cross (Rom. 3:23; 6:23; Isa. 59:2; 1 Tim. 2:5; 1 Pet. 3:18).

- Wiccans believe that experience is a more important revelation than any code of belief, and it's more important to reveal your own truth than to rely on doctrine. Christians believe that the most important revelation of truth is the Bible (Ps. 119:47, 72, 97; 2 Tim. 3:16; Heb. 4:12).

- Wiccans worship the earth and creation. They recognize the divinity of nature and all living things.[10] Christians believe in worshipping the Creator not the creation (Deut. 4:39; Rom. 1:25; Jude 25).

- Wiccans believe that people have their own divine nature: "Thou art Goddess, thou art God."[11] Christians believe that even though we are created in God's image, humanity is still sinful and fallen (Gen. 1:26–27; Rom. 5:12). The Bible clearly teaches that all kinds of wickedness come from within a person not divinity (Jer. 17:9; Mark 7:14–23).

- Wiccans do not believe that Jesus was God in the flesh or Creator of the universe. They view Jesus as "a great white witch who knew the Coven of Thirteen."[12] The key principle that sets Christianity apart from any other religion is the belief that Jesus is God. One of the names for Jesus in the Bible is Immanuel—which means "God with us" (Matt. 1:21–23; John 1:1, 14, 18; 8:24; Phil. 2:5–6).

Think about It

1. Review what God specifically says about the subject of witchcraft in the Bible.
- Deuteronomy 18:9–13
- 2 Kings 9:22
- Micah 5:12
- Nahum 3:4
- Revelation 21:8

2. For teenagers what's the attraction with Wicca? Why?

3. How is Wicca similar to Christianity? How is Wicca different?

4. What is the goal of Wicca and witchcraft?

5. Do you have a friend or family member who is messing around with Wicca or witchcraft? Besides praying for this person, how else does God want you to help him or her?

Chapter Nine

Jehovah's Witnesses

There's a good chance you have seen them on a street or in a park distributing their magazine, *The Watchtower.* Or perhaps a couple of men or women, maybe with some children, have come to your door wanting to talk with you about God. They call themselves Jehovah's Witnesses.

The Jehovah's Witnesses have reaped great benefits from its ties with celebrities like the Jacksons—although superstar Michael Jackson left the church many years ago. Rapper Ja Rule was also raised in this religion. Tennis superstars Venus and Serena Williams are very active Witnesses.

Active, baptized Witnesses ("peaks") spend billions of people hours each year spreading their beliefs in different parts of the globe. They conduct millions of "Bible studies" each year for those who express interest in their doctrines. *The Watchtower,* a semi-magazine, has a circulation of more than 20 million in 126 different languages. The Watchtower Society's publishing arm is aggressive in its goal to oppose and contradict biblical doctrines and teaching. There are also millions of people in the United States who attend Watchtower memorial conventions each year. These people are not "peaks"; they are only sympathetic supporters of the group.

The History of the Jehovah's Witnesses

Charles Taze Russell founded the group we now call the Jehovah's Witnesses. He was born February 16, 1852, in Pennsylvania. As a teenager he rejected the views of the Trinity and hell taught by the Congregational church that he was attending. He thought these doctrines were unreasonable. For awhile he was a skeptic and condemned "organized religions."

In 1870, at the age of eighteen, Russell formed a Bible study group and started developing his own system of theology, with heavy emphasis on the Second Coming of Christ. Six years later Russell was "elected" pastor of the group. In 1879, Russell left this "church" over his position on the atonement of Christ and launched his own magazine—eventually known as *The Watchtower*. It was about this time that Russell set 1914 as the year for the Battle of Armageddon— when God would wipe out the governments of the world and establish His kingdom.

In 1884, "Pastor" Russell incorporated Zion's Watch Tower Tract Society in Pittsburgh, Pennsylvania. Two years later the Society published the first of six books of Russell's, now part of the series entitled "Studies in the Scriptures." Russell described the series as "practically the Bible itself." His lack of any formal theological training and his turbulent career landed him in court in 1912, charged as a perjurer. Russell claimed that he knew the Greek alphabet, but under close examination he couldn't even read Greek letters.

The Watchtower Bible and Tract Society (WTBTS), which Russell founded, was up and running by 1896. He moved his headquarters from Pennsylvania to Brooklyn, New York, in 1908. Watchtower headquarters are still in Brooklyn today, where they have, among other things, a huge printing plant, modern apartment buildings and offices, and "Gilead"—a Bible school.

At the start of World War I in 1914, Russell claimed that it was "the beginning of the end." But Armageddon never happened that year or even in the following year. Russell, a failed "prophet," died in 1916.

The seventh book in the "Studies in the Scriptures" series was compiled from Russell's writings and published after his death. It was this seventh volume, "The Finished Mystery," that caused a split in the organization. In 1917, the larger group followed a man named J. F. Rutherford, while the smaller group kept on by itself. The smaller group became known as the Dawn Bible Students Association.

As the new president, Joseph F. Rutherford—former legal advisor to the WTBTS—introduced many changes in the organization. He also set 1925 as the new date for Armageddon, which the Society publicized in *The Watchtower* as not being from man but of God and "absolutely and unqualifiedly correct."[1] Even though 1925 came and went—with no Armageddon—Rutherford kept pressing ahead, saying that he was misunderstood. In 1931, the Society got a new name—the Jehovah's Witnesses. The name came from Isaiah 43:10 (KJV): "Ye are my witnesses, saith [Jehovah]." The name Jehovah doesn't actually appear in the Bible. It's an English version of the Hebrew consonants JHVH, which Old Testament writers used to refer to the Lord God. Rutherford wanted the new name to avoid confusion between the WTBTS and other groups that had split off.

Rutherford was also responsible for innovating something the JWs are famous for—the door-to-door visitation strategy. This was started to increase membership—one of Rutherford's main goals—so the word was spread that only 144,000 people were going to make it to heaven. The idea of only 144,000 going to heaven is a result of a wrong interpretation of Revelation 7:4–8, which talks about the twelve tribes of Israel.

But as the 1930s arrived, the WBTBS had a big problem. Membership was growing rapidly, and soon there would be 144,000—plus, Armageddon still hadn't happened. No problem; Rutherford had a solution. He announced that everyone who had become a JW prior to 1935 would go to heaven (the "little flock") while everyone else who became a JW after that would become part of the "great crowd." These people would not go to heaven, but instead would live on earth in a new paradise after Armageddon and the millennium.[2]

The JWs kept growing in numbers and influence in spite of Rutherford's scornful criticisms of Christianity. Even though they didn't set any more dates, *The Watchtower* and Rutherford kept saying that Armageddon was "coming soon." In 1941, the WTBTS said that there were "just a few remaining months until Armageddon." Followers were even told not to marry or have babies; instead, they should spend the remaining time doing kingdom work. Rutherford died in 1942, and still there had been no Armageddon.

Nathan Knorr, the next WTBTS president, preferred to stay more in the background than his predecessor. One of the first policy changes Knorr made was to make all future Watchtower publications anonymous. The first step in coming up with a new dating system for the end times was the release of a book entitled *The Truth Shall Make You Free* in 1943. The new Watchtower revelation contradicted one from Charles T. Russell, when he had said that Jesus had returned invisibly in 1874. This time the Watchtower said that Jesus actually returned invisibly in 1914 and the generation that had been alive then would not "pass away" (Matt. 24:34) before Armageddon occurred.

Of course time marched on and there was still no Armageddon, so once again Watchtower leaders had to do some readjusting and shuffling of dates, revising some of their teaching. While Knorr was president, a new system of dating was installed—this was the absolute and final one—because the date for Armageddon was 1975. This system worked out perfectly for all the JWs who had been alive in 1914. Once again followers were encouraged not to marry, have babies, or go to college; they should spend the remaining time doing kingdom work.

These people sure had a hard time with dates!

The year 1975 arrived right on schedule but not Armageddon. Knorr now joined ranks with his predecessors Russell and Rutherford as a failed prophet. Nonetheless, Knorr still accomplished much during his reign as president, including increases in world missions and publishing many new JW textbooks and doctrinal teachings. Probably the most significant thing Knorr published during this time was the New World Translation of the Bible. Despite his failure as a prophet and a huge number of people who deserted the WTBTS, when Knorr died in 1977, there were still more than 2 million active JW members worldwide.

Frederick Franz—a former vice president who was supposedly the most knowledgeable Hebrew scholar in the Watchtower organization—followed Knorr's presidency. But Franz had a clouded past, much like Russell's. More than twenty years before he became president, he was questioned in the *Douglas Walsh v. the Right Honorable James Latham* trial in Scotland. At one point he confessed that he couldn't translate a simple verse—Genesis 2:4—from English to Hebrew—thus committing perjury. This was after he claimed that he was very knowledgeable in many languages, including Hebrew and Greek.

Franz, like Knorr, had to navigate the Watchtower organization through a variety of storms—including the 1975 failed prophecy. His excuse to JWs was a familiar one—people had misunderstood the statements in publications about Armageddon because they had not really been attempting to set a specific date. Even though Franz didn't set any new specific dates, he continued to teach that people alive in 1914 would absolutely experience Armageddon. But JWs were quickly running out of time for the 1914 generation when Franz died at age ninety-nine in 1992.

Wanting to bring an end to this lingering date problem, Knorr's successor, Milton G. Henschel, got rid of the whole 1914 generation prophecy and created more "new light" (a convenient JW term to explain away their frequent changes in their teachings). Now instead of this prophecy applying only to those alive in 1914, it now applied to all citizens of earth—in any generation—who would see the signs of Christ's coming but not change the way they lived.

Despite all the changes that have occurred in the history of the Jehovah's Witnesses, one thing remains the same. The foundation from which they teach still comes from the theology of their founder—Charles T. Russell—who was a master at perverting the Bible to say whatever he wanted it to say. JWs consistently try to distance themselves from his teaching; they even made a statement in an issue of *Awake!* magazine that they don't publish his teachings or quote him as an authority. All of Russell's positions—denial of the Trinity, Jesus being God and being resurrected physically, the Holy Spirit being God and having a personality, hell being a place of eternal punishment, and Jehovah's Witnesses as the only religion having the truth—are all still currently taught by JWs.

The Watchtower Society

The Jehovah's Witnesses are convinced that God Himself personally established the Watchtower Society. Witnesses believe that God meant for it to be His visible representative on earth, supposedly teaching the Bible to humanity through this organization and no other. According to Jehovah's Witnesses, people cannot determine the meaning of Scripture without the Watchtower Society and its enormous amounts of literature. *The Watchtower* magazine has done a great job of reminding people of this concept for generations, using statements such as "Jehovah's organization has a visible part on earth which represents the Lord and is under his direct supervision."[3]

The Watchtower Society believes it exercises authority over all true believers because Jehovah's Witnesses are God's visible image on earth. Witnesses are expected to obey the Society as the voice of God—whose instructions are communicated through JW literature.[4] Witnesses are taught to obey the Society without question. Its authority supercedes all others', including the government's. An example of this is if a young man is drafted into the military, he must obey the Society and refuse to serve in the military.

Also, according to Jehovah's Witnesses, the teachings of the Watchtower Society should affect every dimension of an individual's life. Here are some examples from issues of *The Watchtower* magazine:

- The Society is "an organization to direct the minds of God's people."[5]
- "Jehovah's organization should influence our every decision."[6]
- "We must recognize not only Jehovah God as our Father but his organization as our Mother."[7]
- "Unless we are in touch with this channel of communication that God is using, we will not progress along the road to life, no matter how much Bible reading that we do."[8]

It's amazing how far they go with their church authority—acknowledging the Society as "mother" and saying that reading the Bible without JW interpretation isn't adequate to learn the things of God. Individuals are warned to only depend on the Watchtower literature for use in interpreting the Bible. Witnesses are taught to surrender their minds to the Society and "not to think" for themselves when it comes to understanding the Bible. The following excerpts are examples of this type of "encouragement":

- "God has not arranged for His Word to speak independently or to shine forth life-giving truths by itself. It is through his organization God provides this light."[9]
- "Avoid independent thinking . . . questioning the counsel that is provided by God's visible organization."[10]
- "Fight against independent thinking."[11]
- "We should seek for dependent Bible study, rather than for independent Bible study."[12]

The Watchtower Society has claimed to be God's prophet on earth all through its history. Knowing this, it's interesting that the Society now admits it was wrong in numerous prophecies, including the 1874 prediction of the Second Coming of Christ, its 1925 prediction of the coming of select Old Testament saints to earth, and its 1975 prediction of the end of human history. What happened to all the "enlightenment and direction" that Jehovah's Witnesses were supposed to be receiving from the Society?

Concerning the control the Watchtower Society has over the way so many people think, we should heed the following warning from the Bible about listening to wrong advice: "Be careful that no one takes you captive through philosophy and empty deceit based on human tradition, based on the elemental forces of the world, and not based on Christ" (Col. 2:8).

The New World Translation

The Jehovah's Witnesses have their own version of the Bible called the New World Translation (NWT). It presents evident biases, including eliminating any trace of Jesus Christ's association with God the Father.

Consider the following side-by-side comparison of Colossians 2:9 in the New International Version and the New World Translation:

New International Version	New World Translation
For in Christ all the <u>fullness of the Deity</u> lives in bodily form.	Because it is in him that all the <u>fullness of the divine quality</u> dwells bodily.

When you compare the words that have been underlined in each version, you can see the obvious bias.

When making a case for their faith, Witnesses like to use familiar, or even popular, terminology, especially when it can be twisted to serve their purposes. One example is the phrase *born again*. The phrase is found in John 3:3: "Jesus replied, 'I assure you: Unless someone is born again, he cannot see the kingdom of God.'"

Here's how the Jehovah's Witnesses define *born again* on page 48 of their textbook *Make Sure of All Things*: "Born again means a birth-like realization of prospects and hopes for spirit life by resurrection to heaven. Such a realization is brought about through the water of God's truth in the Bible and God's holy spirit, his active force."[13]

This definition is totally different from what the New Testament is actually teaching about spiritual birth. The phrase *born again* literally means "born from above." Jesus is saying that the Holy Spirit must spiritually transform us. This new birth is something that only God can give us as believers (2 Cor. 5:17; Titus 3:5; 1 Pet. 1:3; 1 John 2:29). Being born again also carries the idea of becoming a child of God by trusting in His name (John 1:12–13). There is no verse in either the Old or New Testament that even comes close to what the Jehovah's Witnesses are saying in their definition of being born again. This is only one example of many demonstrating how they twist and pervert what the Bible really teaches.

Well-respected, legitimate biblical scholars have concluded that the NWT is not only biased, it is dishonest in some places. British scholar H. H. Rowley said: "From beginning to end this volume is a shining example of how the Bible should not be translated. It's an insult to God."[14]

It's interesting that the Watchtower Society has always been hesitant to identify members of the New World Translation committee. Supposedly it was because the members wanted to stay anonymous so that God would get all the glory. But it also kept scholars from checking credentials and protected the translation committee from being held accountable for mistakes. Not surprisingly, when the translation committee members were finally revealed, it turned out that none of them were qualified to do this kind of work. Not only did the members not know Hebrew and Greek (the original languages of the Old and New Testaments), but most of them only had a high school education.

Considering the misapplications and misinterpretations Jehovah's Witnesses have made of the Bible in the NWT, we should ask ourselves how well we personally know the Bible. Do we know it well enough to recognize when the Jehovah's Witnesses pervert a verse or twist a word? If you're still not convinced, the following statement by W. J. Schnell, a former member of the Watchtower Society, underscores how important it is to really know and understand the Bible: "The Watchtower leadership sensed that within the midst of Christendom were millions of professing Christians who were not well grounded in 'the truths once delivered to the saints,' and who would rather easily be pried loose from churches and led into a new and revitalized Watchtower organization."

It's scary to think that millions of copies of the New World Translation are printed and distributed each year by the Watchtower Society. Unfortunately, most Jehovah's Witnesses will never hear the truth about the translation that carries so much weight in their lives. Jesus said, "You will know the truth, and the truth will set you free" (John 8:32). How well do you know God's Word? One of the most important things you can do is to commit yourself to being a serious student of the Bible and learn how to accurately apply it to your daily life (Heb. 4:12).

What Do Jehovah's Witnesses Believe?

The Jehovah's Witnesses have been described as a cult—like the Mormons and other religious groups. *Webster's Dictionary* defines a cult as a religion that is seen as unorthodox or spurious. Basically it means that people think it is a perversion of the original. A cult can also be defined as a group of people who have gathered around a specific person's misinterpretation of the Bible. The Mormons followed Joseph Smith and Brigham Young's spiritual ideas. The Jehovah's Witnesses have mainly followed the teachings of Charles T. Russell and J. F. Rutherford.

Jehovah's Witnesses don't believe in celebrating holidays like Christmas, Easter, or Thanksgiving. They also don't believe in celebrating birthdays. Witnesses don't vote, salute the flag, or serve in the military. People who do these things get kicked out of the church.

I visited their official Web site and looked at the section titled "What Jehovah's Witnesses Believe." Below are some of the beliefs listed:

- God's name is Jehovah.
- Christ is God's son and inferior to Him. Jesus was the first of God's creations.
- Christ died on a stake not a cross.
- Jesus was raised from the dead as an immortal spirit person.
- The earth will never be destroyed or depopulated.
- God will eliminate the present system of things in the battle of Armageddon.
- The wicked will be eternally destroyed. Hell is mankind's common grave.
- The human soul ceases to exist at death.
- Only a little flock of 144,000 go to heaven to rule with Christ.
- Taking blood into the body through the mouth or veins violates God's laws.

They also believe that the Holy Spirit is neither a person nor God but instead is God's "active force." And they do not believe in the Trinity, seeing it as a satanic doctrine rooted in ancient paganism. There is one solitary being from all eternity, Jehovah God, the Creator and Preserver of the universe and of all things visible and invisible.

Key Differences
between Jehovah's Witnesses and Christians

There are many significant differences between what Jehovah's Witnesses and Christians believe. Here are some of the important ones:

- JWs believe that there is only one God; they do not believe in the Trinity. Christians believe that God is three totally coequal and eternal Persons who exist as one divine Being (Matt. 3:13–17; 2 Cor. 13:14).

- JWs believe that Jesus is God's Son and is inferior to Him. Christians believe that Jesus is divine, the second person of the Trinity (John 1:1; Col. 1:1–19; Phil. 2:5–11).

- JWs believe that Jesus was not raised bodily from the grave but as a spirit. Christians believe that Jesus did rise physically from the grave and showed Himself to many people (John 20:24–29; Luke 24:36–43).

- JWs believe that the earth will never be destroyed. Christians believe heaven and earth will "pass away" and that God will create new heavens and a new earth (Matt. 24:35; Isa. 65:17).

- JWs are taught to refrain from independent thinking and to strictly adhere to the decisions, guidance, and scriptural understanding of the Watchtower Society. Christians depend on guidance from the Holy Spirit as they study the Bible and learn to obey God, not other people (Acts 5:29; 17:11; 1 John 2:26–27).

- JWs believe that you can work for your salvation because of Christ's death. Christians believe that Jesus' death on the cross totally paid for all of humanity's sins and that salvation is a result of God's grace and is a free gift from Him (Rom. 3:24–25; 5:12–19; 1 Pet. 2:24).

- JWs believe that man does not have an immortal soul and that at death man's life force (spirit) leaves and no longer exists. Christians believe that man has an immortal and eternal soul (spirit) that at death goes to one of two places: to be with Jesus or to wait for judgment (Luke 23:46; 2 Cor. 5:8; Phil. 1:22–23; John 5:24–30).

- JWs believe that Jesus invisibly returned to earth in 1914 and now rules from heaven. Christians believe that Jesus will return to earth physically and clearly (1 Thess. 4:1–17).

Think about It

1. What one thing do you find most interesting about the Jehovah's Witnesses? The thing most confusing about their religion?

2. What do you think attracts people to become Jehovah's Witnesses?

3. When you have the opportunity to talk with a Jehovah's Witness about your relationship with Jesus, keep in mind the following things:

- Make sure that you really know what the Bible teaches about the Trinity, the deity of Jesus and His resurrection, who the Holy Spirit is, and that salvation is a free gift by God's grace, not something you can work for.
- The most important thing is to go beyond logic or reason and to know in your heart that Jesus is truly God and that He died for your sins and was physically raised after three days and is alive today.

Chapter Ten

Satanism and the Occult

I t was my first trip to Poundridge, New York, home to celebrities
such as David Letterman and Mariah Carey. In comparison, it
makes Beverly Hills look small. I had been invited to speak at a
"town hall" type meeting regarding satanic and occultic activities
going on in the public school. The other speakers included federal
law enforcement officials, a Catholic priest, a concerned parent from
the area, an educator, and a minister from the Midwest who had produced videotape on the subject.

The audience that night was a mixture of age, race, and personal
opinions regarding the use of satanic and occultic practices in the
classroom. At times there seemed to be a shouting match going on
between those on the stage and those in the audience. After the pre-
sentations were over, I had the chance to talk with several people,
including a high school student named Justin.

I've seen a lot of "body mod" in my travels, but Justin's was
definitely beyond the norm. The longer we talked, the harder it was
for me to concentrate on what he was saying because of his multiple
piercings, many of which were occultic symbols. He also had a silver
rod as big around as a pencil that went through the bottom of his
nose and hooked around both sides with sharp pointed ends. (I won-
dered what the poor guy did when he got a cold.) But what amazed
me most was the car antenna he had attached to his shoulder. I
wanted to ask him if he used it to contact the International Space
Station or aliens from another planet, but out of respect for him and
our discussion, I refrained.

Justin approached me to talk about spirituality and his religion.
He was a practicing Satanist, and he wanted to make sure I knew that

Satanism isn't about taking drugs or harming children and animals. "Satanism respects and exalts life," he said. "Uniqueness and creativity are encouraged, not mindless conformity."

Justin went on to explain that Satanists believe that good and evil are merely terms that some people twist to suit their own purposes, that in the end each person must make the final judgment about right and wrong. For Satanists, Satan is a symbol of the power of that choice. Justin said what really matters is that you are a mature, sensitive, self-aware individualist who revels in the Darkness and who wants to connect with others who believe the same way. "A Satanist challenges that which is presumed to be true," he said. Confident that he had made his case with me, Justin walked off into the night.

In his mind I'm sure he feels that he has a good grasp of Satanism, but I'm not sure he fully understands what he is ultimately involved in. Justin is like a lot of teenagers I meet who are exploring spirituality and looking for the freedom to preserve true individuality and creativity.

Let's examine Satanism and the occult more carefully and see how they relate to Christianity.

What Is Satanism?

Oftentimes we can't pick a Satanist out of the crowd. There's no certain way that they dress although sometimes they do wear black cloaks and pentagrams. They work out in the gym, listen to a variety of music, and even work at some ordinary jobs. But it's what they believe that sets them apart.

Defining Satanism is no easy task. The Satanism 101 Web site says it has been called the "unreligion" because it does not subscribe to the notion of a deity with human form or attributes nor a being who must be worshipped. Anton LaVey, author of *The Satanic Bible,* says, "Satanists are born, not made."[1]

In Satanism, Satan is considered the prototype, or original pattern, to be followed. He represents certain qualities that the Satanist embodies, such as the questioning of all, the avoidance of oppressive thinking, the determination toward success and human potential, and the regard for a rational self-interest. Satanism embraces numerous cultural and religious ideas and concepts from ancient Rome and Greece, Zoroastrianism, the Aztecs, Hinduism, the Egyptians, and others. Basically, a Satanist accepts Satan as a life principle concept worth following.

Even though Satanists are free to choose how and what characteristics of Satan they imitate, there are nine satanic statements from *The Satanic Bible* that most would agree with and follow.

1. Satan represents indulgence, instead of abstinence!
2. Satan represents vital existence, instead of spiritual pipe dreams!
3. Satan represents undefiled wisdom, instead of hypocritical self-deceit!
4. Satan represents kindness to those who deserve it, instead of love wasted on ingrates!
5. Satan represents vengeance, instead of turning the other cheek!
6. Satan represents responsibility to the responsible, instead of concern for psychic vampires!
7. Satan represents man as just another animal, sometimes better, more often worse than those that walk on all fours, which, because of his "divine spiritual and intellectual development," has become the most vicious animal of all!
8. Satan represents all of the so-called sins, as they all lead to physical, mental, or emotional gratification!
9. Satan has been the best friend the church ever had, as he has kept it in business all these years![2]

Satanists also consider "The Eleven Satanic Rules of the Earth," written by Anton LaVey, to be important guidelines to pursue.

1. Do not give opinions or advice unless you are asked.
2. Do not tell your troubles to others unless you are sure that they want to hear them.
3. When in another's lair, show him respect or else do not go there.
4. If a guest in your lair annoys you, treat him cruelly and without mercy.
5. Do not make sexual advances unless you are given the mating signal.
6. Do not take that which does not belong to you unless it is a burden to the person and he cries out to be relieved.
7. Acknowledge the power of magic if you have used it successfully to obtain your desires. If you deny the power of magic after having called upon it with success, you will lose all you have obtained.
8. Do not complain about anything to which you need not subject yourself.

9. Do not harm little children.

10. Do not kill nonhuman animals unless attacked or for your food.

11. When walking in open territory, bother no one. If someone bothers you, ask him to stop. If he does not stop, destroy him.[3]

Satanists have an interesting way of thinking. On one hand they say that they don't believe in Satan; yet, Satan is the one whom they are trying to imitate and the one they want to follow. It doesn't make much sense.

Satanists also frequently say, "Hail Satan!" This can be interpreted in two ways. First, it is an acknowledgment of Satan's achievements, his heritage, and his character. It is also another way of saying, "Hail me!" since Satanists imitate the qualities of the devil himself, and he is the one who began the lie that we can be the god of our world and live independent of God.

Therefore, since Satan is really at the heart of Satanism, let's look at how the Bible describes him.

Who Is Satan?

Satan has done a masterful job of confusing us about his true identity. Movies, books, games, song lyrics, and celebrities often misrepresent Satan as other than he truly is. It is easy to get the wrong idea about Satan and, in the process, lose sight of the intensity of the spiritual battle in which we are all engaged.

Usually Satan is portrayed in one of two ways. Sometimes he is pictured as a goofy little buffoon with horns on top of his head, wearing a red suit, carrying a strange-looking pitchfork, and running around poking people. Every Halloween I see little kids dressed according to this portrayal of the devil.

Satan is also portrayed in the other extreme: as a horrible-looking creature that is part human, part monster, and part alien, complete with bulging eyes, fire for breath, and the most hideously evil laugh imaginable. Slasher movies and computer games are filled with these images, and even CD covers and comic books depict Satan in this way.

Satan has used these and other imaginative pictures of himself to confuse and disarm us. It's no wonder so many people today don't take him seriously or, in the case of Satanists, don't understand whom it is they are following. Satan's strategy is working quite well.

In a national survey, George Barna asked, "Is the devil for real?" Of those who responded, 70 percent said that Satan does not exist, that he is simply a symbol used to signify evil.[4] Satan would like nothing better than for people to be deceived into believing that he doesn't exist. After all, if Satan isn't real, then we don't have to be concerned about spiritual warfare—and we lose.

That's why it's important to rely on what the Bible says. God's Word is the ultimate source of truth. It confirms the reality of Satan and gives us an accurate picture of his true character.

Ezekiel 28 tells us much about Satan, including the following:

- "You were the seal of perfection, full of wisdom and perfect in beauty." (v. 12)
- "From the day you were created you were blameless in your ways until wickedness was found in you." (v. 15)
- "Your heart became proud because of your beauty; For the sake of your splendor you corrupted your wisdom. So I threw you down to the earth; I made a spectacle of you before kings." (v. 17)

Satan's incredible pride led him to rebel against God. He refused to accept the fact that all of his greatness came from God. As his pride grew, he determined to take over God's kingdom and seize control of His power. Satan—the most beautiful, the most powerful, and the wisest of all created beings—plunged all of creation into a deadly spiritual war. Yet it is a war he can never win.

Because of God's awesome holiness, He cannot tolerate rebellion and evil. God stripped Satan of his position of authority, drove him from heaven, and made a disgrace of him as He threw him to earth. Though this battle between God and Satan started in heaven, we are now caught in the middle of it on earth. Because of Satan's great hatred and anger toward God, he also hates those of us who try to live in a way that pleases the Lord. We become the targets of his fierce attacks. But God is still in control. Satan can only go as far as God permits.

The Character of Satan

Now that we know more about Satan's true identity, it will be helpful to know more about his character. Even though Satan in his present fallen state retains a great deal of power, he still has limitations.

The names given to Satan give insight into his characteristics, background, and activities. Here's a brief look at the names of Satan, their meaning, and some of the places in the Bible where each is used.

Name	Meaning	Location
Satan	Adversary/opposer	Zech. 3:1; Matt. 4:10; Rev. 12:9; 20:2
Devil	Slanderer	Matt. 4:1; Eph. 4:27
Evil one	Intrinsically evil	John 17:15; 1 John 5:18–19
Serpent	Craftiness	Gen. 3:1; 2 Cor. 11:3
Ancient serpent	Deceiver in Eden	Rev. 12:9
Dragon	Fierce nature	Rev. 12:3, 7, 9
Abaddon	Destruction	Rev. 9:11
Apollyon	Destroyer	Rev. 9:11
Adversary	Opponent	1 Pet. 5:8
Accuser of our brothers	Opposes believers before God	Rev. 12:10
Tempter	Entices people to sin	Matt. 4:3; 1 Thess. 3:5
Ruler of this world	Rules world system	John 12:31
The spirit now working in the disobedient		Eph. 2:2
Beelzebul	Chief of the demons	Luke 11:15
Belial	Worthlessness; wickedness	2 Cor. 6:15
God of this age	Controls philosophy of the world	2 Cor. 4:4
Ruler of the (atmospheric domain)	Control of unbelievers	Eph. 2:2
Father of liars	Perverts the truth	John 8:44
Murderer	Leads people to eternal death	John 8:44
Angel of light		2 Cor. 11:14

Satan is also described in 1 Peter 5:8 as a roaring lion, looking for someone to devour. You might say that he's like a serial killer stalking his next victim. But if we have a relationship with Jesus, there is no reason to live in constant fear of what Satan might do next. God has not given us a spirit of fear but rather one of power (2 Tim. 1:7). In 1 John 4:4 we are told that "the One who is in you is greater than the one who is in the world." It's easy to start believing Satan's lies about his power—especially when we see so much wickedness all around us. Evil is obviously more powerful than we are in our humanity. However, the Bible reminds us that God is stronger yet. He is almighty and all-powerful. God will conquer all evil—including the devil himself. Satan is a created being and is no match for God. When we have a personal relationship with Jesus, we can have victory over the attacks of the devil.

The Strategies of Satan

Because Satan was created above all others in intelligence, he is a brilliant war planner and has developed some deceptive strategies to use in his attacks against us. Part of his overall plan includes doubt, difficulties, self-sufficiency, false teaching, and confusion.

We must never underestimate our enemy or the forces of darkness. The devil has a plan and a purpose for everyone. For those who don't have a relationship with Christ, he will do all he can to keep them from putting their faith and trust in Jesus as Savior and Lord of their lives. He doesn't care how much people go to church, youth group activities, or Christian concerts—just as long as they don't put their faith and trust in Jesus.

Satan's plan for those who have decided to become a Christian is to keep them from growing in the strength and knowledge that comes as a result of following Jesus. He also wants to keep them from telling others how they can obtain forgiveness, hope, and love in a relationship with Christ.

In spite of all this, the good news is ours: Jesus is our defender and He defeated Satan on the cross. Colossians 2:15 tells us that Jesus disarmed the powers and authorities, making a spectacle of them and triumphing over them by the cross. The devil is powerless in the presence of the Son of God. Ultimately, Satan will be judged and cast into the lake of fire for eternity (Rev. 20:7–10).

We are on the winning side when we know Jesus personally. God has given us all the necessary resources to withstand the attacks of the enemy, including special spiritual weaponry and equipment. Our strategy for victory is summed up in James 4:7: "Therefore, submit to God. But resist the Devil, and he will flee from you."

What Is the Occult?

John Edward exhibited psychic abilities from an extremely early age and was deemed "special" by many in his family. John is now a psychic medium, author, and lecturer who claims to have helped thousands over the last fifteen years with his ability to predict future events and communicate with those who have crossed over to the "other side." He is currently hosting the increasingly popular TV show *Crossing Over.* What most people don't realize is that John uses occult practices to "help" people.

The word *occult* comes from the Latin word *occultus,* which means "hidden." Ironically, very little about the occult remains secret anymore. The activities, beliefs, practices, and rituals that have been traditionally considered occultic are now well documented and published. Anyone can go to the library, a bookstore, or online to find information on occultic activities.

There is little agreement as to what is occult, but for the purposes of this book, let's use the following definition from the Ontario Consultants on Religious Tolerance: "The Occult is a set of mostly unrelated divination and/or spiritual practices or activities which appear to tap into forces that have not been explained by science, and which are not conventional practices seen in traditional religions."[5]

Occultic practices are sometimes separated into three main categories: divination, magic, and religious and spiritual pursuits.

Divination

Divination includes various techniques of predicting the future.

- *Astrology:* The idea that your future is determined by the precise location of the sun, moon, and planets at the time of your birth.
- *I Ching:* An ancient Chinese oracle book that some believe can be used to answer questions and predict the future. A number from 1 to 64 is generated by casting dice, coins, or by selecting sticks. The oracle book applies different meanings to each of the possible numbers.
- *Numerology:* The routine of assigning a numeral to each letter in a person's name, then obtaining a series of numbers

that have special meaning to the individual. The primary purpose of numerology is character analysis—to discover what "the above has to say to us below."

- *Palm reading:* The practice of using the creases in your palm and the shape of your fingers to predict your future.
- *Runes:* Method that typically uses a group of letters (approximately 16 to 31, but usually 26) from an ancient Northern European alphabet. These letters are inscribed on pieces of plastic, paper, or on small rocks. A group is tossed, and the future is predicted from the runes that land inverted and those not upturned, as well as from their position.
- *Scrying:* A technique that involves gazing into a bowl of water, a black mirror, hot coals from a fire, or a crystal ball to produce visions of the future.
- *Tarot cards:* A type of fortune telling that uses a set of 78 Tarot cards. The cards are interpreted according to their inherent meaning, as modified by the importance of their position. The set of cards can be divided into four suites: wands, cups, pentacles, and swords. In each suite there are number cards (ace to 10), a king, a queen, a knight, and a knave. There are also an additional 22 cards that form the greater "arcana." These include the High Priestess, Hanged Man, Reaper, Enchantress, Sarcophagus, Devil, Juggler, Death, and so on. The cards are shuffled, then a few are dealt and arranged in a specific formation—such as a circle, cross, square, and so forth—and interpreted. Ultimately, the Tarot is supposed to show how to overcome shortcomings and enter into enlightenment.
- *Teacup reading:* Shapes formed by tea leaves, after a cup of tea has been consumed, are used to predict the future.

Many other methods, including dice, dream interpretation, playing cards, pendulum movements, and dominos, are also used to foretell future events.

Magic

This category of occultic activity involves practicing different kinds of rituals and spells, as well as ceremonial magic in a variety of ways. These are all used to change the environment and the material world in order to reach the objectives of the magician.

Religious and Spiritual Pursuits

A collection of unrelated alternative religions are also sometimes considered occultic. These include:

- Syncretistic religions from the Caribbean, such as Vodun and Santeria
- Satanism and Wicca
- Eastern religions, such as Hinduism, Buddhism, and Taoism

Those involved in occultic activities see it as fascinating, harmless, mysterious, spiritual, and even a great source of healing power and knowledge. But there's another perspective that's important for us to consider—God's.

What Does the Bible Say about the Occult?

The Bible leaves little doubt concerning how God feels about occultic practices. Here are a few verses that reflect God's attitude toward them.

- Leviticus 19:26: "You are not to practice divination or sorcery [fortune-telling and witchcraft]."
- Leviticus 19:31: "Do not turn to mediums or consult spiritists, or you will be defiled by them; I am the LORD your God."
- Leviticus 20:27: "A man or a woman who is a medium or a spiritist must be put to death. They are to be stoned; their blood is on their own hands."
- Deuteronomy 18:10–11: "No one among you is to make his son or daughter pass through the fire, practice divination, tell fortunes, interpret omens, practice sorcery, cast spells, consult a medium or a familiar spirit, or inquire of the dead."
- 2 Kings 21:6: "He [King Manasseh] made his son pass through the fire, practiced witchcraft and divination, and consulted mediums and spiritists. He did a great amount of evil in the LORD's sight, provoking [Him]."

Even though we may be naturally curious about things like astrology, horoscopes, fortune-telling, witchcraft, and other bizarre practices, we must remember that Satan is behind them. A lot of our interest and fascination comes as a result of wanting to know and control the future. However, in the Bible, God tells us everything that we need to know about what is going to happen in the future.

The information received through occultic practices will be distorted and unreliable because of the bad source: Satan and demons. Yet we can always trust the guidance we receive through the Holy Spirit and the Bible. Since God created us, He knows what is best for us and will never mislead or confuse us. We simply must put all of our confidence in Him and trust Him completely.

Check out God's advice in Proverbs 3:5–6: "Trust in the LORD with all your heart, and do not rely on your own understanding; think about Him in all your ways, and He will guide you on the right paths." We don't need to figure out everything on our own. We need to listen for God's voice and watch for His direction everywhere we go and in everything we do.

If you're still not convinced because trusting in God seems so limiting and restrictive in this present age of freedom and tolerance, then check out what the Bible says about occultic practices in Isaiah 8:19: "When they say to you, 'Consult the spirits of the dead and the spiritists who chirp and mutter,' shouldn't a people consult their God? [Should they consult] the dead on behalf of the living?"

Think logically for a minute: why consult with witches and mediums that are trying to get answers from dead people? It makes much more sense to go to the living God for answers. Because God is eternal, He has already been to the future. Don't let anyone or anything take you away from the living and true God.

Key Differences
between Satanism, the Occult, and Christianity

There are many significant differences between what Satanists, Occultists, and Christians believe. Here are some of the important ones.

- Satanists believe that Satan is the prototype, the original pattern to be followed. Basically they accept Satan as a life principle concept worth following. Christians believe that Jesus is our example; He is the one we need to emulate. Jesus Himself said, "Follow Me" (1 Cor. 11:1; Mark 8:34).
- Satanists believe they must acknowledge the power of magic as a way to obtain their desires. To deny the power of magic after having called upon it with success will result in the loss of all they have obtained. Christians believe that power is received from the Holy Spirit of God. God gives us the

desires of our hearts when we delight ourselves in Him (Acts 1:8; Ps. 37:4).

- Satanists call theirs the "unreligion" because it does not subscribe to the notion of a deity with human form or attributes, nor a being who must be worshipped. In other words, they have no personal God. Christians believe in a personal God who is self-existent, all-powerful, all-knowing, and who never changes (Job 42:1–6; Ps. 115:3; Mal. 3:6; Matt. 19:26).

- Occultists believe in practicing things like astrology, I Ching, palm reading, and scrying to answer questions about life and to predict the future. Christians believe that no one knows the future except God, and therefore we need to trust in Him. He has plans to give us hope and a future (Eccles. 8:7; Prov. 3:5–6; Isa. 41:23; Jer. 29:11).

- Occultists believe in using witchcraft, interpreting omens, telling the future based on signs, conjuring spells, and communicating with the dead. Christians believe that participating in any of these things is a sin and detestable in God's eyes (Deut. 18:10–12).

Think about It

1. Have you ever known anyone who was deeply involved in Satanism or the occult? How could you help them?

2. What strategy does the devil most often use in your life? Why? What does God want you to do in this situation to achieve victory?

3. List some specific examples of confusing messages you have noticed in the world. How can you best prepare yourself to be on guard against these subtle attacks?

Chapter Eleven

What Will You Do with Jesus?

After speaking at a girls' unit in the Los Angeles County juvenile hall about how to have a relationship with Jesus, I sat down to chat with one of the girls. "Y'all think this Jesus is Lord and King. But I know better," she blurted out. "He ain't nothin' but a homeboy. He's just like the other homeys on my street and in my neighborhood." This girl had no clue who Jesus really is, and yet He's the only One who can help her straighten out her life.

Another time I was speaking to a group of youth workers on the subject of reaching the generation of today. As we discussed the most effective way to tell teenagers about Jesus, I reminded those in attendance how important it was not to reduce the Lord to something less than who He really is. I went on to say that in our attempts to show how Jesus can relate to students, we have gone too far with things like "Hip-hop Jesus" or "Jesus Punk" or even "Jesus the Homeboy." The Bible—God's Word—reminds us that Jesus Christ transcends all, and He is already incredibly relevant to the lives of people of all ages and cultures.

One of the youth pastors in the audience spoke up and said that he totally disagreed with what I was saying. He explained that the only Jesus kids in his neighborhood would accept is "Jesus the homeboy." And before he could even share Jesus with his kids, he needed to help them feel good about themselves culturally.

I couldn't believe what I was hearing. No wonder it's so hard for people to understand who Jesus really is when that's what they are being taught! Jesus isn't a hip-hop dude, a rapper, or a homeboy. He's the Son of God. The only way young people will ever feel good about themselves—culturally or otherwise—is when they find their true identity in Christ. I agree that when we share the story of Jesus, we must be culturally sensitive, but we must never reduce Jesus to someone less than who He truly is.

Maybe you've already come to the conclusion that Jesus is more than a homeboy, but do you know Him as Lord of lords and King of kings? One of the most important factors in cutting through all the religious confusion of our relative-truth world is to really know the One you've placed your faith and trust in, the One who conquered death and made a new life possible.

Since much of what we know about Jesus is revealed to us in the Bible, let's first examine the evidence that it truly is the Word of God.

The Bible

Skylar's been struggling with understanding where the Bible came from—especially when trying to explain it to her friends at school. Over and over again the question keeps coming up: "How do we know that someone didn't just make up the Bible?"

In 2 Timothy 3:16 we read that "All Scripture is inspired by God and is profitable for teaching, for rebuking, for correcting, for training in righteousness." The Bible is "inspired" by God. *Inspiration* can be defined as the mysterious process by which God worked through human writers, employing their individual personalities and styles to produce divinely authoritative and inerrant writings.[1] The Bible is free from any errors in its original writings.

But be careful in how you use and understand the term *inspiration.* Usually we think of a singer, author, or artist being "inspired" in their work, which means we think it's really good. But when this same word is applied to the Bible, it has a different meaning. The Bible has been "breathed" by God. The Bible claims to be His very Word: it has come from His mouth.[2] No other religious book has ever made this claim. The authors of the Bible—most of them prophets—spoke God's words. A prophet was someone who was supposed to say exactly what God told him to say (Jer. 26:2; Exod. 4:30). Although God didn't verbally dictate the Bible to each author, the end result is as precise as if He had. God supernaturally supervised what they wrote but allowed them to use their own vocabulary and style.

The Bible is the most unique book ever written. It's the written

Word of God. The Bible was written over a fifteen-hundred-year span of time by forty-four different authors (all living in different places) in three different languages (Hebrew, Aramaic, and Greek) on three different continents (Asia, Africa, and Europe). It's an amazing book in its unity in the middle of its vast diversity. It presents one continuous drama from Genesis to Revelation—the rescue of humanity. It has a central theme—the Person of Jesus Christ. From beginning to end, the Bible has one unified message—humanity's problem is sin and the remedy is found in Jesus. All this evidence points to the idea that there was one mind behind the writing of God's Word, the Bible.

The uniqueness of the Bible's message can be summed up in Romans 6:23: "For the wages of sin is death, but the gift of God is eternal life in Christ Jesus our Lord." Christianity teaches that all people are spiritually dead and there is no hope that we can fix ourselves. Other religions say the opposite. They agree there is something wrong spiritually, but they hold out hope that somehow, through some kind of human effort, we can be fixed. The Bible makes it clear that spiritually dead people can't fix themselves (Eph. 2:8–9). And because God is holy, He cannot have a relationship with sinful people. The problem is that we all have sinned (Rom. 3:23).

But even though we have this horrible spiritual condition, there is good news—God has a remedy. We can have eternal life, not only some continued existence on another spiritual plane after death. We can actually have fellowship with God Himself (John 17:3). No other religion in the world promises us eternal life and closeness with the living God (Heb. 4:16). And it starts in this life—the moment we place our faith and trust in Jesus Christ. Finally, the Bible's message is unique because eternal life is a free gift. It's not a gift that can be earned—it can only be received. We can have this gift by admitting our need for life because of our spiritual death, and then relying on the work that Jesus did for us by paying the penalty for our sin.

No other book ever written has had the kind of circulation as the Bible. Billions of copies have been sold and distributed around the world. The Bible was also one of the first important books ever translated. According to the United Bible Societies, the Bible and portions of it have now been translated into more than 2,200 languages.

The Bible is also unique in its ability to have survived, over the course of time, through criticism and persecution. It actually has more ancient manuscript evidence to support it than any ten pieces of classical literature combined.[3] Throughout history, people have tried to burn and outlaw the Bible. Others have spent their lives trying to refute it—even so-called scholars. Yet the Bible has endured all its enemies and has stood up even to the most persistent critics.

When tested by the same criteria as other historical manuscripts, the Bible demonstrates incredible accuracy for the historical events it reports. For example, did you know that there are 5,656 partial and complete manuscript portions (in Greek) of the New Testament alone? In comparison, the next closest historical manuscript is Homer's *Iliad*, with only 643 copies. There is also supporting evidence from early Christian writers outside the Bible, including Clement of Rome, Ignatius, and Polycarp. There is even support from non-Christian historical writers, such as Tacitus and Josephus.

The Bible also made incredible statements about the earth, the heavens, and the body that predated their "scientific" discoveries by two thousand to three thousand years. Consider what the Bible says about the concept of allowing the ground to remain unplowed and unused during every seventh year (Exod. 23:10–11). Scientists have now discovered that this concept was accurate and way ahead of its time.

In the 1840s, pregnant women had a one in six rate of dying from "childbirth fever" if they went to a particular hospital in Vienna, Austria. Dr. Ignaz Semmelweis noticed something in common about their deaths. Doctors who had just completed autopsies on victims of "childbirth fever" had examined all the women who died. So Dr. Semmelweis implemented a new policy that required all doctors to wash their hands after performing an autopsy. As a result, the death rate among pregnant women dropped radically to one in eighty-four. What's significant about this story is that God set down cleanliness laws through Moses 3,500 years before Dr. Semmelweis even existed (Num. 19:17, 19).

There is archaeological evidence that supports the Bible as well. Two of many examples are the Elba tablets, discovered in northern Syria, that support the Creation account in Genesis 1-11 and records found in the famous hanging gardens of Babylon that indicate the accuracy of 2 Kings 25:27–30 where Jehoiachin and his five sons were given a monthly ration and a place to live and were well treated. Well-known archaeologist Nelson Glueck said, "It may be stated categorically that no archaeological discovery has ever controverted a biblical reference. Scores of archaeological findings have been made that conform in clear outline or exact detail to historical statements in the Bible."[4] There can be no question as to the historical reliability of the Bible.

The Bible is also unique because it is the only book in the world ever written that offered specific predictions about the future hundreds of years before they were literally fulfilled. A lot of these predictions focus on the first and second comings of Christ. There are several unique things about prophecies in the Bible in contrast to other attempts made to predict future events:

- The prophecies were very specific.
- None of the predictions have ever failed.
- Since the prophecies about Christ were written hundreds of years before His birth, no one could have been making intelligent guesses.
- Many of these predictions were beyond human ability to somehow force their fulfillment.

Other books claim divine inspiration—such as the Koran, the Book of Mormon, and parts of the (Hindu) Veda—but none of those books contain predictive prophecy that is completely accurate.[5] Hundreds of predictions in the Bible—at times given hundreds of years in advance—have been literally fulfilled. Fulfilled prophecy is another glaring sign of the unique divine authority of the Bible.

The Bible is our ultimate source of truth. It doesn't make any sense why anyone would want to base his or her eternal destiny—and life on the planet—on someone's opinion when we have God's Word, the Bible, available to help us and guide us. The core message of the Bible, which sets it apart from any other book in all of history, is the offer of the free gift of eternal life through Jesus Christ.

So, Who Is Jesus?

Jesus is still the most controversial person who has ever lived. For centuries people have been confused about Him, and many still are today. Try asking people at school or in your neighborhood, "Who do you think Jesus is?" and you'll get lots of different answers. Yet this is the most crucial question in life. The way we answer this question will spell the difference between life and death, the difference between a meaningful life and a meaningless one.

Jesus asked this very question of His followers. Let's look at the answers He got. In Matthew 16, we read about the following discussion:

When Jesus came to the region of Caesarea Philippi, He
asked His disciples, "Who do people say that the Son of
Man is?" And they said, "Some say John the Baptist; others, Elijah; still others, Jeremiah or one of the prophets."
"But you," He asked them, "who do you say that I am?"
Simon Peter answered, "You are the Messiah, the Son of
the living God!" (vv. 13–16)

Initially the disciples answered Jesus' question with the common
view people held—that Jesus was one of the great prophets who was
brought back to life. However, Peter acknowledged Jesus as the
promised and long-awaited Messiah. If Jesus were to ask you this
question, how would you answer? Is He your Savior and Lord?

There are two things that we all must be absolutely sure about if
we are going to live the kind of life God designed for us to live as
Christians. We must know who Jesus is, and we must know what He
did.

What Did Jesus Do?

Almost two thousand years ago Jesus entered the human race.
He was born in a barn in a small Jewish town to a poor working-class
family. He never wrote a book, had a family, or went to college. He
never traveled more than two hundred miles from His birthplace and
only lived to be thirty-three years old. Yet despite His rather humble
existence, Jesus lived the most influential life of anyone—ever.

Jesus was the most unique person who ever lived. He was both
completely God and completely man. Some specific aspects of His
life set Him apart from everyone else.

No one ever said the things Jesus said. He claimed that He was God
(John 8:19; 10:30; 14:9). He also said that He had the authority to
forgive sins for eternity (Mark 2:1–12) and that He was the only way
to God (John 14:6).

No one ever lived as Jesus lived. He was born of a virgin (Matt.
1:20) and had no home or income. He healed the sick and gave sight
to the blind (Mark 1:33–34; John 9). His life was perfect and without sin (Heb. 4:15). He suffered unjust opposition, an unfair trial,
and undeserved execution. Yet He lived to give us life abundantly
and eternally (John 10:10, 28). Jesus Christ was the perfect model
for the rest of humanity concerning what it means to be totally
dependent on God. Now no one can ever say to God, "You don't
understand." Jesus experienced it all. Some might argue that

Buddha, Marx, and Muhammad also lived similar lives, but none truly compare with the life of Jesus.

No one in all of history has ever had the influence Jesus has had. His impact has been special. More than one-third of the people in the world admit to being His followers. No faith has ever had as many followers. Without a doubt He is the greatest person who has ever lived. Napoleon, while he was imprisoned on St. Helena, had this to say about Jesus:

> Alexander, Caesar, Charlemagne and myself have founded great empires, but on what did those creations of our genius rest? Upon force. But Jesus founded his on love. This very day millions would die for him. I have inspired multitudes with enthusiastic devotion: they would die for me. But to do it, I had to be present with the electric influence of my looks, my words, my voice. When I saw men and spoke to them, I lit up the flame of devotion in their hearts. But Jesus Christ by some mysterious influence, even through the lapse of eighteen centuries, so draws the hearts of men towards him that thousands at a word would rush through fire and flood for him, not counting their lives dear to themselves.[6]

Certainly Muhammad also has had a great influence, but his lifestyle was very different from that of Jesus. From its beginning Muhammad's religion was militaristic. He attacked passing caravans for their valuables and wiped out the Jewish tribe of Banu Quraiza after the battle of Khandaq in AD 627. Although there are some exceptions of moderate peace-loving Islamic countries, in many parts of the world today Islam remains the religion of force. A vivid demonstration of this fact was the attacks on the World Trade Center and the Pentagon. Some might argue that there have been some representatives of Christianity who have also committed some horrible acts, but Jesus didn't. He refused the way of force and embraced the way of love. Besides His inspiration for purity, care for others, and generosity, the greatest example of Jesus' life of love was His death on the cross. It was self-sacrificing, unconditional love for His enemies.

No one ever taught as Jesus taught. He taught as one who had authority and not like the religious teachers of the day (Matt. 7:29). Jesus never quoted other authorities when He taught. His teaching went deep and was powerful. Look at some of the other things that made Jesus' teaching unique:

- He never taught anything that was wrong.
- The wisdom with which He taught was awesome, yet he never went to college.
- No one has ever been able to improve on His moral teachings, even up to the present.
- His teaching is relevant to all people in every culture.

Jesus' behavior also matched His teaching. This is something that has never been equaled. Confucius, Muhammad, Buddha, and even Mother Teresa have taught some good things, but none of these great leaders ever managed to completely live what they taught. Jesus taught the highest standards, and He kept them all.

No one ever died as Jesus died. He suffered many things and was crucified on a cross. But His death on the cross was different from others' (Mark 8:31). Jesus suffered the punishment *we* deserved; He took on the sins of the world (Isa. 53:6). He was our substitute (Rom. 5:8). Jesus dealt with human evil like no other religious leader ever did.

Human evil won't go away. It's been around since the very first man and woman. It's on your campus, on TV, in the newspaper, or maybe even in your own family—it's everywhere. Jesus is the only One who has the answer to the problem of human evil—it's a heart problem. "For from within, out of people's hearts, come evil thoughts, sexual immoralities, thefts, murders, adulteries, greed, evil actions, deceit, lewdness, stinginess, blasphemy, pride, and foolishness. All these evil things come from within and defile a person" (Mark 7:21–23). People don't have good hearts, like some religions want us to believe.

Because God is holy, He must judge evil. The consequence for sin—evil—is death (Rom. 6:23). However, because God is love, He reaches out to the sinner in a powerful way. "But God proves His own love for us in that while we were still sinners Christ died for us!" (Rom. 5:8). God more than justly dealt with human evil: He paid the penalty for it Himself. Christ offered a single sacrifice—for all time and for everyone who would ever live. Jesus, like no other religious teacher or leader, offers complete forgiveness and a brand-new life.

Finally, no one ever rose from the dead as Jesus did. After His death, His body was placed in a tomb and sealed (Mark 15:46–47). Three days later His followers went to the tomb and found it empty (Matt. 28:5–7). After His resurrection, Jesus showed Himself to many people and gave them convincing proof that He was alive (Acts 1:3).

Jesus was resurrected in time and space by the supernatural power of God. By conquering death, Jesus proved He was who He claimed to be. This becomes the major reason why we should believe the Christian view of heaven and hell over Islam, Buddhism, Hinduism, or any other religion.

It was one thing for Jesus to make promises about life after death, as other religious leaders have, but it was quite another issue for Him to validate this claim by rising from the dead after three days. Muhammad died at sixty-two and did nothing to validate his claims about life after death. He remained dead and his bones still lie in Medina. Buddha's bones were divided up and are currently enshrined in several different countries. The tomb of Jesus is empty, and His bones are not found in a memorial somewhere to be viewed. Jesus is alive, and His resurrection from the grave is what began the entire Christian movement. Because Jesus is alive, we can know Him personally and enjoy a relationship with Him in this life, and we can be confident of spending eternity with Him. Jesus has changed my life, and He can change yours as well.

Joan Osborne received seven Grammy nominations for a song she wrote entitled "One of Us." The song's lyrics were a reflection of someone trying to make sense out of who God is and what He is like. In the chorus she asks the question, "What if God was one of us?" Unfortunately for Joan—and many others like her in our world today—it appears that no one has ever taken the time to tell her that God did become one of us in the person of Jesus Christ. This is the most awesome truth in history! God was actually "speaking our language" in Jesus and showed us how much He cares for us.

In Mark Twain's classic novel *The Prince and the Pauper,* King Henry's son—the prince—temporarily exchanged places with a boy living on the streets. He wanted to see what it was like to be a very poor person. Jesus voluntarily chose to step down from heaven and empty Himself of all His rights as the Son of God to become the unique God-man. He was not half God and half man but rather fully God and fully man. This is what makes Christianity more than a religion; it is unique and relevant because God actually became one of us. Jesus is unique among religious leaders because He not only claimed to bring God into our world in His own person but He also made good on that claim with powerful evidence.

Literary giant Daniel Webster, from whom we got the dictionary, was attending a dinner meeting with a group of other literary scholars in Boston. The dinner conversation eventually turned to a discussion about Christianity. Webster spoke openly about his belief in Jesus as the Son of God and his dependence on Christ's death on the cross for the forgiveness of his sins. One of the other dinner guests spoke up, "Mr. Webster, can you really comprehend how Jesus can be both man and God?" Webster replied, "No sir, I cannot. If I could understand it, He would be no greater than myself. I believe that I need a super-human Savior!"

What about you? Just because you can't fully understand something about God doesn't mean that it's false. There is an element of mystery to God becoming a man—human flesh and bones—without ceasing to be what He eternally was—God. One of the greatest mistakes we could make is to think that we could fully understand this concept. Isn't it amazing that when we put our faith and trust in Jesus, this supernatural mystery seems to fade.

To fully understand the uniqueness of Jesus and how He makes Christianity stand out from all other religions in the world, we not only need to know that God became one of us, but we also need to know why. Couldn't He have accomplished the same thing in another way—like writing a message across the sky for everyone to read or through an infomercial on late-night TV or how about a Web site?

The problem is that none of these methods of communication could accomplish all that had to be done to enable us to have a restored relationship with God. There are three reasons why Jesus became one of us: (1) to reveal God to us, (2) to give us a pattern for living, and (3) to pay the penalty for our sin.

1. *Jesus became one of us to reveal God to us.* Jesus is the physical representation of the invisible God (Col. 1:15–20; Heb. 1:1–13). He showed us everything about God's character that can be expressed in human terms—in a way we could see and touch. In the Bible are several accounts of Jesus existing as God and as man. For example, in one situation Jesus was alone, praying, after sending His followers off in a boat. The Bible never mentions God praying because He doesn't need prayer—He's self-sufficient. By praying, Jesus showed Himself to be a man. Yet, after He finished praying, Jesus walked across the lake to join His disciples. When Peter, one of the disciples, tried to walk to Jesus on the water, he took a few steps and started sinking—he couldn't pull it off. Jesus pulled Peter safely back into the boat and all the disciples responded, "Truly You are the Son of

God!" (Matt. 14:22–33). Only man prays, and only God walks on water—Jesus did both!

Because Jesus is fully God, we need nothing else. The Bible teaches that in Him we are made complete (Col. 2:10). Are you relying on all the resources that are yours in Jesus?

2. *Jesus became one of us to give us a pattern for living.* The Bible tells us that He had a relatively normal life growing up (Luke 2:52). He experienced pain, thirst, hunger, fatigue, pleasure, rest, and ultimately death. Jesus set a pattern for us that we wouldn't normally have had. However, there was one exception to His normal life—even though He was fully man, Jesus never sinned (Heb. 4:15). As a man, Jesus experienced all the trials and temptations of life, and He gave us a great example to follow (Matt. 4:1–11). Not only did He demonstrate how to live life to the fullest (John 10:10), but because He is God, He offers us the power to follow His example.

3. *Jesus became one of us to pay the penalty for our sin.* We were not created by God to be robots that would automatically love and obey Him. God gave us free will—the freedom to choose. Our human nature caused us to choose to disobey God and go our own way. Trying to live our lives without God is the very core of sin. The Bible teaches that our sins have cut us off from God (Isa. 59:2). This results in a severed relationship with God. The only remedy for this problem of separation was Jesus' death on the cross. He paid the penalty for our sin and bridged the gap between God and us (1 Tim. 2:5–6).

If Jesus had not become one of us, we would have no savior because sin requires death for its payment. Because God does not die, the Savior had to be human in order to be able to die. However, the death of an ordinary man would not pay for sin eternally, so the Savior must also be God. As a man Jesus could die, but only as God could His death have infinite value—sufficient to provide payment for the sins of the whole world. Christ suffered once for all our sins so that He might bring us to God (1 Pet. 3:18).

God becoming one of us has no meaning without the cross. Jesus' death on the cross made it possible for the entire human race to be brought into a right relationship with God. How awesome! The perfect God-man died a horrific death so that we would not have to face eternal punishment. "For the wages of sin is death, but the gift of God is eternal life in Christ Jesus our Lord" (Rom. 6:23). In Jesus we have total and complete forgiveness. The Hindu doctrine of karma says "You sin, you pay." God says, "You sin, I pay." No other religion makes this possible.

A home for sailors in Liverpool, England, exploded into flames late one night. People caught on the upper floors leaned out the windows, screaming for help. Those who had made it safely out of the building watched helplessly from the street below. Unfortunately, not even the fire escape could reach those who were trapped. The local fire company arrived and quickly pulled a ladder off the truck and pushed it up against the burning building. It was too short. A sailor standing in the crowd rushed up the ladder, carefully balanced on the top rung, and reached up—grabbing the bottom of the window ledge. He yelled, "Quick, scramble over my body and down the ladder to safety." The ladder went a long way, but before anyone could be rescued, it still needed the length of a man. We, too, needed the length of a Man—Jesus—to be rescued from the punishment of our sins.

What Will You Do with Jesus?

There are really only four possibilities of what you can do with Jesus.

1. *You can reject Jesus Christ and His free gift of eternal life.* This is a very serious matter, especially if you do this knowing the issues that are involved and the consequences of this choice. I had an aunt who cursed God on her deathbed and said she wanted nothing to do with Him. I only wish she had changed her mind before she died. You may think that you will have the opportunity to change your mind, but you can't know for sure. Anything could happen and your life could be taken in a moment. If that happened, you would spend eternity separated from God. But I guess my question is, why would anyone want to reject the God who so compassionately loves you and died on a cross for you? Those who steadfastly turn their backs on God and refuse His love, forgiveness, and acceptance have only themselves to blame. The bottom line is that we all must choose, and God will ultimately give us what we want; therefore, we send ourselves to our eternal destiny.

2. *You can put off making a choice about accepting Jesus.* I've talked with some students who say, "I believe what you are saying about Jesus, Steve, but not now. I've got plans for my life and stuff I want to do. God will just get in the way and mess up my plans. I'll deal with Jesus when I'm old and don't have much time left." Stop and

think about the potential consequences of putting off this decision. I met James in a prison in Canada. While still a high school student, he had attended one of our citywide campaigns in eastern Canada three years before. Unfortunately, for the last two and one-half years he had been in prison. His mom found out that I was coming back to the area, told James, and he asked her to get in touch with me. So on the way back from the airport, we stopped at the prison where he was incarcerated.

My friend Peter and I were ushered into a small secured visiting area while a guard went to get James. As he sat down across the table from me, I asked James if he remembered who I was. I'll never forget his response. "Of course I know who you are, Steve. Your words have haunted me for the past three years." I asked him what he was talking about. "When you were speaking at the Rideau Regional Centre and you told the audience how to establish a relationship with Jesus, I pretty much blew you off 'cuz I had more important things to do. I wish now that I had never left that building without Jesus. My life's been a mess ever since." The fantastic news is that less than thirty minutes after I arrived at that prison, James surrendered his life to Jesus. James and I talked for quite awhile about how much pain and trouble he would have avoided had he not put off his decision to receive Christ. When you realize the suffering that Jesus willingly went through for you, the only proper response should be to say yes to Him. Putting off your decision about Jesus may also be unwise because of what we read in Isaiah 55:6: "Seek the LORD while He may be found; call to Him while He is near." The longer you put off your decision about Jesus, the harder your heart will become and the more difficult the choice.

3. *The wisest decision is to surrender your life totally and completely to Jesus,* to respond to His awesome love for you by putting your faith and trust in Him, coming to the point in your life when you decide you want a living, intimate relationship with Jesus as your Savior and Lord. Revelation 3:20 describes how Jesus takes the initiative and waits for us to respond: "Listen! I stand at the door and knock. If anyone hears My voice and opens the door, I will come in to him and have dinner with him, and he with Me." Jesus will only come into our lives by personal invitation. He will never force Himself on us. I saw a great illustration of this promise in an art gallery in Europe. The picture I saw is famous and was painted by an artist named Holman Hunt. It's a picture of a small house with a long

vine growing up the door, which has no handle. Standing outside the door is Jesus, holding a small lantern and wearing a white robe with a red cloak. On His head is a crown of thorns, and His hand knocking on the door is nail-pierced. Because there is no handle on the outside of the door, it obviously can only be opened from the inside.

The picture is an incredible illustration of our lives. Jesus stands patiently knocking, waiting for us to "open the door." Jesus promises to come into our lives if we will invite Him. We don't have to understand everything about following Jesus or even "clean up our act." But we do need to consider the cost. To follow Jesus will cost you your favorite—and hidden—sins. It will cost you your self-centeredness as well. The more you grow in your relationship with Jesus, the more areas of your life you will need to surrender to Him. You may even lose some friends as you "go public" with your relationship with Christ. But as you think about it and weigh the cost of being a Christian, you also need to check out the benefits. It's much more than only a ticket to heaven. "What no eye has seen and no ear has heard, and what has never come into a man's heart, is what God has prepared for those who love Him" (1 Cor. 2:9). We can't even begin to imagine all that God has in store for us in this life and for eternity. If you have never surrendered your life to Jesus, *stop,* and go back to chapter 2, "What Does It Mean to Be a Christian?" and find the section on "Steps to Peace with God." Take a few minutes to surrender your life to Jesus—you'll never regret it.

4. There is yet another possibility left of what you can do with Jesus: *neglect Him.* If you have already put your faith and trust in Him—established a relationship with Him—are you spending the necessary time with Him to grow spiritually? The most important time in our day is the time we spend alone with God. As we grow in our relationship with God, we are better equipped to face problems in life. Make it a priority to spend time each day alone with God. When we consistently study the Bible and pray, God gives us direction and wisdom for our lives, as well as strength and peace to deal with the issues of life.

As you get to know Jesus, you can't help but love Him. And the more you love Him, the more you will want to obey Him. But all this takes time. Start by changing your priorities.

Think about some of your other relationships. If you never spent any time with your friends and family, what kind of relationships would you have? You know those people because you spend time with them. The same is true with Jesus. Take time to get to know Jesus, and I guarantee you'll never be the same.

Everything about Jesus and what He accomplished was unique. He did things that Muhammad, Buddha, Confucius, and others could not. Jesus is definitely special. What will you do with Him?

Think about It

1. What is the difference between knowing about Jesus and really knowing Him? Be specific.

2. Who first told you about Jesus? How was He described to you? What about Him did you find appealing at first? What about now?

3. What areas of your life are the most difficult to surrender to God? Why?

4. Explain in your own words how Jesus is unique and different from other religious leaders. What makes Him so special?

Chapter Twelve

How Do I Tell My Friends in Other Religions about Jesus?

Nicole sent me an e-mail out of concern for a friend. She explained how one of her girlfriends seemed to be totally consumed by Wicca. "She doesn't see the danger or even how much her involvement in Wicca is changing her," Brenda said. "I want to help her so badly, but I don't know what to do. Where do I start?" Josh waited to talk with me personally about a buddy of his. "Russo, I've got this friend who's a Mormon. How do I help him understand the truth about his religion and about Jesus?"

What can we do to help those we care about who are involved in a religion that does not believe that Jesus is God? All around us are friends, family members, neighbors, and people at school who are living in spiritual darkness. The devil has done a masterful job of getting them to believe his lies: "the god of this age has blinded the minds of the unbelievers so they cannot see the light of the gospel of the glory of Christ, who is the image of God" (2 Cor. 4:4).

They have bought the lie of religion that says you have to work your way to heaven. Let's face it, that's an easy trap to fall into. We are so used to earning things, working for things. Even as little children we are taught that if we do a certain thing, we will be rewarded. We then want to carry this over to religion. It's hard to imagine that something as significant as eternal life is a free gift from God. Of course Satan complicates matters with his lies, and unfortunately, many people believe him. You and I have the privilege of rescuing these spiritual hostages of the enemy (2 Tim. 2:26).

Practical Tips

To rescue someone from spiritual darkness, we must first fully understand the level of commitment and preparation that must be in place in our own lives. Like all good soldiers, we must be prepared for battle. Let's look at twelve practical things we need to remember as we talk about Jesus to our friends who are involved in other religions.

1. *Approach your friends gradually.* Be patient and take them one step at a time closer to an understanding of what it means to have a relationship with Jesus

2. *Determine what unmet need in their lives seems to be met in the other religion.* This can be a starting point for telling them how Jesus has met this need in your life—or someone else's—and how He can do the same for them.

3. *Be sensitive to your friends' perspective.* Don't make fun of their religion, as illogical as it may seem. This will only cause them to avoid discussing their religion with you.

4. *Try to find common ground with them.* Ask questions about their religion to see what might be similar to Christianity. Establishing common ground can be a great starting point for discussion. Some similarities might include:

- living a moral life
- finding personal peace
- the importance of self-discipline
- having compassion for others who are less fortunate
- the importance of prayer and meditation

5. *Highlight the differences between their religion and Christianity.* Most people in other religions have never really heard the truth about what Christians believe.

6. *Clarify religious terms and definitions.* For example, the term *born again* to a Hindu would be referring to reincarnation. To a Christian it means being spiritually transformed.

7. *Model your trust in God alone.* Help your friends see that the only source of security, acceptance, and significance in this world is found in a relationship with Jesus Christ.

8. *Be open about your faith in a personal God, not some "force" out there.* Emphasize the benefits of a personal God:

- He is able to love us.
- He can hear and answer our prayers.
- He can sympathize with our pain.

9. *Clearly explain the issue of sin and the opportunity we have for forgiveness.* No other religion offers complete and total forgiveness for sin as does Christianity. Jesus is the only religious leader who died for our sin on a cross and rose again.

10. *Use the Bible frequently to explain and support what you believe.* Make sure personal study of the Bible is a priority in your life. Unfortunately, most Christians are not equipped to respond biblically when cult members or people from other religions mentioned in this book show up on their doorstep.

11. *Pray with your friends*—with their permission.

12. *Focus on Jesus.* It all comes down to who you believe Jesus is—that's why it's important to point to Him as much as possible. Help your friends see that He is more than a prophet, a good teacher, or just a man. He is God. Help your friends understand that

- Muhammad and Jesus both can't be right.
- Buddha and Jesus both can't be right.
- Joseph Smith and Jesus both can't be right.
- Charles Taze Russell and Jesus both can't be right.
- The "god" and the "goddess" and Jesus all can't be right.

Encourage your friend to read the New Testament Books of Luke and John, so they learn more about the life and work of Jesus. Jesus is unique; there is no other religious leader like Him—never has been and never will be. If we have a relationship with Jesus, we have been given the awesome responsibility to tell others the good news of salvation through Him. It is singularly the most important information in history because it offers the truth of the only door to heaven. Jesus said, "I am the way, the truth, and the life. No one comes to the Father except through Me" (John 14:6).

God Uses People Like You

Throughout history God has used people like you to change the course of history. Have you ever asked God to use you as a light in the darkness of your home, neighborhood, campus, and in your world? No matter how old you are or what weaknesses you may have, don't let anyone ever put you down or make you feel incapable of being used by God. Instead, remember what the Bible says in 1 Timothy 4:12: "No one should despise your youth; instead, you should be an example to the believers in speech, in conduct, in love, in faith, in purity."

I owe my life to someone like you, and that's why I'm so committed to helping teenagers be all that God designed them to be. Robbie was taking drum lessons from me while I was in the music industry. Each week during his lesson he would tell me about his best friend. He told me how he shared everything with this friend, but he never told me his best friend's name. I actually started to become jealous of Robbie and this relationship he had with his best friend because I didn't have a friend like he had. One day, before a drum lesson, I finally asked Robbie what his best friend's name was, and his response about knocked me over! "Jesus," Rob said. "And He can be your best friend also." Not long after that I met Robbie's aunt and uncle, Billy and Danielle—who were Christians and entertainers in Hollywood—and they helped me put my faith and trust in Jesus.

As a result of one teenager's courage to tell me about his "best friend," people across the United States and in eighteen foreign countries have heard the message of God's love through our ministry.

God used a teenager in my life, and He wants to use you, too, no matter what your age. As you become aware of different issues troubling those around you, ask God how He wants to use you to help that person find answers in a relationship with God. Jesus said, "You are the light of the world. A city situated on a hill cannot be hidden. No one lights a lamp and puts it under a basket, but rather on a lampstand, and it gives light for all who are in the house. In the same way, let your light shine before men, so that they may see your good works and give glory to your Father in heaven" (Matt. 5:14–16). One person really can make a difference in their world!

A Candle in the Dark

In Romania in December of 1989, Communist authorities sent police to arrest Laszlo Tokes, the pastor of the Hungarian Reformed Church in the town of Timisoara. But when they arrived, the police found a solid wall of people blocking the entrance to the church. Members of many different churches had joined together in protest. The people didn't budge for the police. They held their ground the entire day and into the night. Shortly after midnight, a nineteen-year-old student named Daniel Gavra pulled out a packet of candles. Lighting one, he passed it to the person next to him.

Then he lit another candle and another one after that. One by one the brightly shining candles were passed out among the crowd. Very soon the light of hundreds of candles pierced the darkness of that cold December night. Christians came together in unity, disregarding denominational differences and joining hands in the pastor's defense. Even though the crowd stayed through the night and the next day, the police finally broke through and arrested the pastor and his family.

But that was not the end. The religious protest led to political protest in the city as people moved to the town square to begin a full-scale demonstration against the Communist government. Once again Daniel passed out candles. Ultimately troops were brought in to squelch the demonstration. Hundreds of demonstrators were shot, and Daniel's leg was blown off. Yet despite the opposition, their example inspired the whole nation of Romania and ultimately caused the collapse of the evil dictator Ceausescu.

One young man lit the candle that would eventually light up a whole country! It only takes a small flame in a dark world to make a difference. Will you be the first candle in the dark in your home, on your campus, or in your community?

Think about It

1. What are the three most meaningful things you learned in this book? How do they apply to your life?

2. Think of at least one person you know who needs to be rescued from spiritual darkness. Take a few minutes to pray for that person, asking God how He wants to use you. Then think about what might be the best strategy you can use to reach him or her.

Fifteen Essentials of Christianity

1. The Bible

- "Inspired" by God and free from any errors in its original writings (2 Tim. 3:16).
- Written over a fifteen-hundred-year span of time by forty-four different authors (all living in different places) in three different languages (Hebrew, Aramaic, and Greek) on three different continents (Asia, Africa, and Europe).
- It actually has more ancient manuscript evidence to support it than any ten pieces of classical literature combined.
- No unconditional prophecy of the Bible about events to the present day has gone unfilled.

2. God

- God is all-powerful (Job 42:2; Ps. 115:3; Jer. 32:17; Matt. 19:26).
- God knows everything (Ps. 139:1–6; Isa. 46:9–10; John 2:25).
- He does not change or vary (Ps. 102:27; Heb. 13:8; James 1:17).
- He is holy (Exod. 15:11; Ps. 24:3; Isa. 40:25; Hab. 1:13).
- God has no beginning and has no end (Deut. 33:27; Isa. 44:6; 57:15).
- God is not limited; He is infinite (1 Kings 8:27; 2 Chron. 2:6; Ps. 147:5; Jer. 23:24; Acts 17:24–28).
- God is separate from His creation, is the source of all life, and is self-existing (Isa. 57:15).
- God is completely present everywhere (Ps. 139:7–12; Jer. 23:23–24).

- God is a spirit (John 1:18; 4:24; 1 Tim. 1:17; 6:15–16).
- God is love (Hos. 11:4; Jer. 31:3; Mark 1:41; 10:16; 1 John 4:8, 10).
- God is truth (Isa. 44:8–10;; 45:5; Num. 23:19; Rom. 3:3–4; John 14:1, 2, 6; Heb. 6:18; Titus 1:2).

3. The Trinity

- God is eternal and exists in three persons. One God in three persons means one personal God who lives and works in three different ways at the same time.

  God the Father. His holiness demanded that we pay the penalty for our sin, but His love supplied the payment.

  God the Son. He voluntarily sacrificed His own sinless life and intercedes from heaven for us.

  God the Spirit. He lives inside us to help us, to guide us, and to change us.

4. Jesus Christ

- Jesus had a virgin birth (Matt. 1:18; Luke 1:35).
- Jesus was fully God (John 1:1; 1:14; 10:30; Titus 2:13; 1 John 5:20).
- Jesus was fully man and fully human (Heb. 2:16–18; Matt. 1:18; 4:2; Luke 2:40; John 4:6; 8:40; 11:35; 19:28).
- Jesus claimed the authority of God (Mark 2:10; 14:62; John 6:39–40; 10:17–18).
- Jesus is the Creator and the Sustainer (John 1:3; Heb. 1:3; Col. 2:9).
- Jesus had no beginning and has no end (John 8:57–58).
- Jesus is part of the Trinity (John 1:1; Col. 1:15–19; 1 John 5:7–8).
- Jesus is truth (John 1:17; 14:6; 18:37).

5. Holy Spirit

- The Holy Spirit has a will, mind, and feelings—a personality (1 Cor. 2:10–11; Eph. 4:30; 1 Cor. 12:11; Acts 16:6–11).
- The Holy Spirit convicts of sin, performs miracles, intercedes and guides us into truth by hearing, speaking, and showing (John 16:8; Acts 8:39; Rom. 8:26; John 16:13).
- The Holy Spirit is God (Isa. 40:13; 1 Cor. 2:12; Ps. 139:7; Job 33:4; Rom. 8:2; Gal. 5:22; John 14:17).
- The Holy Spirit was the cause of the virgin birth, was involved

in the creation of the world, and was the vehicle in giving us the inspired Bible (Luke 1:35; Gen. 1:2; 2 Pet. 1:21).
- The Holy Spirit is the Counselor and Comforter (John 14:16, 26).
- The Holy Spirit lives inside of believers and will remain in them (John 14:17).
- The Holy Spirit is the one who gives spiritual gifts (1 Cor. 12:1–11).

6. Sin

- Sin originates in the heart and mind of man (Isa. 59:2; Mark 7:21–23; Rom. 1:18–23; 5:12; 3:23; 6:23).
- Sin's two main sides are an active blatant "breaking the law" (1 John 3:4) and a passive "knowing the right thing to do and not doing it" (James 4:17).
- Sin is a failure to conform to the standard of God, or "missing the mark" (Rom. 3:23).
- All people have a sin nature (Rom. 7:14; 17–25; Gal. 3:22; Heb. 3:13).
- Sin is a transgression, or "overstepping" of the law of God (Rom. 4:15; Gal. 3:19).
- Sin is wrongful acts toward God and other people (Exod. 20:1–11, 12–17; Rom. 1:18).
- Temptation is not sin (James 1:14; Matt. 4:1–10).

7. The Death of Christ

- Jesus died in our place—He was our substitute (Isa. 53:5).
- Jesus was the perfect sacrificial offering for our sin. Jesus was the perfect mediator between a holy God and sinful people (Mark 10:45; Rom. 3:25; 5:6–8; Col. 1:20; 1 Tim. 2:5; 1 Pet. 3:18; 2:24; Heb. 4:15).
- God demonstrated His love for us when Jesus died on a cross to pay the penalty for our sins. We have been "bought at a price" (Rom. 5:8; 1 Cor. 6:20).

8. The Resurrection

- Paul writes about the proof of the Resurrection and its prominence in the gospel (1 Cor. 15:3–8).
- Christ's documented appearances after His resurrection, in chronological order:

— Resurrection Sunday: to Mary Magdalene (John 20:14–18); the women coming back from the tomb with the angels' message (Matt. 28:8–10); in the afternoon to Peter (Luke 24:34; 1 Cor. 15:5); toward evening to the disciples on the road to Emmaus (Luke 24:13–31); all the apostles except Thomas (Luke 24:36–43; John 20:19–24).

— Eight days later: to the apostles, including Thomas (John 20:24–29).

— In Galilee: at the Lake of Tiberias to the seven (John 21:1–23); to the apostles and five hundred others on a mountain (1 Cor. 15:6).

— At Jerusalem and Bethany (a second time): to James (1 Cor. 15:7); to the eleven (Matt. 28:16–20; Mark 16:14–20; Luke 24:33–53; Acts 1:3–12).

— To Paul: near Damascus (Acts 9:3–6; 1 Cor. 15:8), in the temple (Acts 22:17–21; 23:11).

— To Stephen outside Jerusalem (Acts 7:55).

— To John on the island of Patmos (Rev. 1:10–19).

9. Salvation

• Salvation is through faith in Christ. Faith, or believing, also involves repentance. To repent means there's been a change of mind and direction—from sin to God. This is a key aspect of salvation (Acts 10:43; 14:23; 16:31).

• When God forgives our sin, canceling debt we could not pay, He does so out of grace (Eph. 2:8–9).

• Salvation is available only through Christ's pain and work (Acts 4:12; Titus 3:5).

• Salvation is a free gift made possible by the undeserved love of God for all who believe and accept His plan (Eph. 2:8–9; John 12:26; 14:1–3; 1 John 3:1–2).

10. Immortality

• The Bible teaches that we have an eternal, immortal soul (Gen. 1:26; 5:1; Job 32:8; Acts 7:59; 1 Cor. 11:7; 15:53–54).

• Believers have been given an immortal inheritance from Jesus (2 Tim. 1:10).

11. Christ's Return

• Jesus promised that He would return to earth for the second time. He said it would be a literal, physical event (Matt. 24:30; Rev. 1:7).

- After His return, Jesus will gather together all the believers—those who have died and the living—to be with Him in His Father's home (John 14:1–3). He will then reward them (1 Thess. 4:13–18; 1 Cor. 4:5; Rev. 22:12).
- Jesus will also judge unbelievers, along with Satan and the powers of darkness; establishing a reign of righteousness and peace (2 Thess. 2:8–10; 1 Cor. 15:23–26; 2 Pet. 3:10–13).
- The exact time of His return would remain unknown. God has set a definite time; it just has not been revealed (Matt. 24:36–44; Mark 13:32–33).
- Jesus' Second Coming should also be an encouragement for us to live the kind of life that honors God—a life of purity (1 John 2:28; 3:3).

12. Heaven

- Heaven is brilliant. It reflects the brilliant glory of God because of His presence (Rev. 21:9–11).
- Heaven has walls and gates (Rev. 21:12–13).
- Heaven has foundation stones (Rev. 21:14).
- Heaven is given measurements in the Bible (Rev. 21:15–18). It is described as being 1,500 miles long, wide, and high.
- Heaven is decorated with brilliant and costly stones (Rev. 21:19–21).
- Heaven is where believers will be for all eternity (1 Thess. 4:17).
- In heaven inhabitants have immediate access to God (Rev. 21:22).

13. Hell

- The final home for those who have rejected Jesus is hell. It is living apart from God—in hostility toward Him—forever.
- Hell is a place of eternal punishment and torment—"weeping and gnashing of teeth." It is also described as "outer darkness" (Matt. 8:12; 13:42).
- Hell is described as the "lake that burns with fire and sulfur" (Rev. 21:8).
- Hell is eternal destruction and exclusion from the face of the Lord (2 Thess. 1:9).
- Hell is also called the "lake of fire" (Rev. 19:20; 20:10). Unbelievers will be cast into the lake of fire at the great white

throne of judgment, and there they will live in torment for eternity (Rev. 20:11–15).

14. The Church

- The concept of the church is unique and very important to Christianity. God purchased the church with the blood of Christ (Acts 20:28).
- The Bible uses several images to describe the church, including the people of God, the body of Christ and the temple of the Holy Spirit (2 Cor. 6:16; 1 Cor. 12:27; Eph. 1:22–23; Acts 2).

15. The Lord's Supper

- Jesus introduced it on the night before He was crucified on the cross (Matt. 26:28; Mark 14:22–24; Luke 22:19–20). He instructed His followers to continue to observe it until His return (Matt. 26:26–29; Mark 14:22–25; Luke 22:14–23).
- The night before He was crucified, as the very first Lord's Supper was celebrated, Jesus gave this command: "Do this in remembrance of Me" (Luke 22:19). The apostle Paul also includes this command in 1 Corinthians 11:24–25.
- The Lord's Supper involves a looking back to the historical event of the cross and an anticipating of His return in the future (1 Cor. 11:26; Matt. 26:29). It is a memorial to the death of Christ. The bread symbolizes His perfect body offered as a sacrifice for sin (1 Cor. 11:24–25; 1 Pet. 2:24). The cup symbolizes Jesus' blood that was shed for forgiveness of sins (Eph. 1:7).
- Participating in the Lord's Supper can be an occasion for spiritual growth.
- Only those who have placed their faith and trust in Jesus should observe the Lord's Supper (1 Cor. 11:27–32).
- The Lord's Supper not only represents the Lord's body; it is also for the body—the church (1 Cor. 11:17–22; 10:17).

Quick Reference Comparison Guide

Islam and Christianity

- Muslims believe there is only one God—Allah. There are to be no partners associated with God. Christians believe in the three persons of the Trinity who are coeternally God, revealed in the Bible as Father, Son, and Holy Spirit (Matt. 3:13–17; 28:19; 2 Cor. 13:14).
- Islam teaches that people are basically good by nature. Christianity says that people are sinful by nature (Rom. 3:12; Eph. 5:8–10).
- Muslims believe that sin is mainly rejecting the right guidance. Sin is serious stuff in Christianity. So serious that it causes spiritual death (Rom. 6:23). It is moral rebellion against a holy God that results in separation from Him. This relationship can only be restored through the shed blood of Jesus Christ (1 Pet. 3:18).
- Muslims believe that salvation is based on human effort and may be gained by having your good deeds outweigh your bad deeds. In Christianity, salvation cannot be earned. It is the free gift of God— a result of His grace and mercy (Eph. 2:8–9). Jesus Christ made this possible by dying for our sins (Rom. 5:8; 1 Cor. 15:3–4).
- Islam teaches that Jesus was a major prophet, below Muhammad, and not God. To even call Him the Son of God is considered blasphemy. Although Muslims do believe in Jesus' virgin birth and that He performed miracles, Christians believe that Jesus is the one and only Son of God, the Savior, the one who died and rose again (Rom. 5:1; 1 Tim. 2:5).

- Muslims believe that the Bible has been corrupted and that the Qur'an is the final word of God. Christians believe that the Bible is authentic, divinely inspired, and the final authority in all matters of truth and faith (2 Tim. 3:16).
- Islam teaches that Jesus did not die on the cross. Instead, He ascended into heaven and Judas actually died in His place on the cross. Muslims believe that it is disrespectful to think that God would allow one of his major prophets to be crucified. Christianity, on the other hand teaches that Jesus died a physical death as our substitute—He died our death. He voluntarily gave His life for us (John 6:51; 10:11–17). After three days, Jesus rose from the grave in bodily form and appeared to hundreds of people (1 Cor. 15). God's main reason for sending Jesus into the world was to die on the cross for our sins (John 3:16; Rom. 8:3; 2 Cor. 5:21; 1 Pet. 1:19–20). The end result of Jesus' death was not dishonor but the highest exaltation (Acts 2:29–33; 5:30–31; Phil. 2:8–11).

Buddhism and Christianity

- Buddhists do not believe in a personal God. Theravada Buddhists believe in nirvana, an abstract void. Mahayana Buddhists also believe in nirvana and in an undifferentiated Buddha spirit. Christians believe in a personal God who is self-existent, all-powerful, all-knowing, and never changing (Job 42:1–6; Ps. 115:3; Mal. 3:6; Matt. 19:26).
- Buddha claimed to point the way to escape suffering and achieve enlightenment. Jesus said He was the way to salvation and eternal life (John 14:6; 5:35).
- Mahayana Buddhists view the physical world as an illusion to be escaped. The Bible teaches that Jesus created the universe, and He called it good (Gen. 1:31; John 1:3).
- The bodhisattvas (Mahayana Buddhists) had to overcome their own sin (self, ignorance, etc.) during the process of being reincarnated through numerous lifetimes. Yet from the very beginning Jesus was without sin. He did not have to go through some kind of process to make Himself sinless (Matt. 27:4; Luke 23:41; 2 Cor. 5:21; Heb. 4:15). For the Christian, salvation comes only through faith in what Christ has done for us (Acts 4:12; Eph. 2:8–9).
- Buddha taught that the way to eliminate suffering was by eliminating desire (Theravada Buddhism). Jesus' answer to end suffering is not to eliminate all desire but to have the right desire

(Matt. 5:6). The Bible does talk about "evil desires" (James 1:13–15) that come from within a person, and these passions (or appetites) tend to get out of control. When we give in to these temptations, we sin. The result of sin is spiritual suffering and death (Rom. 6:23).

- Buddha taught that you must learn to master yourself. The Bible teaches that without God we do not have the strength to control our desires. But through Christ we have strength to do all things (Phil. 4:13) and live successfully.
- Buddhists believe that Jesus was a good teacher but less important than the Buddha. Christians believe that Jesus is the unique Son of God who died for the sins of humanity (Matt. 14:33; John 1:34; Rom. 5:6–8).

Hinduism and Christianity

- Hindus do not believe in a personal God. Instead, they believe in Brahma, an abstract, formless eternal being. Christians believe that God is a personal, spiritual being found in three eternal persons: Father, Son, and Holy Spirit (Matt. 3:13–17; 28:19; 2 Cor. 13:14).
- The Hindu way to enlightenment is from humanity to God and is based on a person's own effort. The biblical way of salvation is just the opposite, going from God to humanity, and is a gift to be received through faith, based on God's grace (Eph. 2:8–9; 1 John 4:10).
- Hinduism offers at least three paths to enlightenment: the way of action and ritual, the way of knowledge and meditation, and the way of devotion. Christianity teaches that there is only one way to salvation: through Jesus Christ (John 14:6).
- Hinduism teaches that humanity's problem is ignorance; Christianity teaches that it's moral rebellion.
- In Hinduism, karma does not affect the relationship with Brahma. In Christianity, sin separates us from God because He is holy (Isa. 59:2).
- In Hinduism the morality, the law of karma, becomes like a law of nature, making forgiveness impossible and consequences inescapable. Because people can forgive and God is a person, God can forgive us for our sins. He has done this through Jesus Christ's death on the cross (Rom. 5:8; 6:23; 1 Pet. 3:18).
- In Hinduism the outcome of enlightenment and liberation is merging into the "Oneness" as the individual disappears. In

Christianity the outcome of salvation is fulfillment and eternal fellowship with God through a loving relationship with Him (John 1:12).

Mormonism and Christianity

• Mormons teach that God the Father is a mere man with flesh and bones. Christians believe that God the Father is spirit and does not have a body of flesh and bones (John 4:24).

• Mormons claim they have received further revelation of biblical teaching in books like *Pearl of Great Price, Doctrine and Covenants,* and the *Book of Mormon.* The Bible makes it very clear that the Bible is the final Word and warns that nothing is to be taken away or added (Rev. 22:18–19).

• Mormons believe that matter is eternal but God is not. Christians believe that God is eternal (Gen. 21:33; Deut. 33:27; Jer. 10:10).

• Mormons teach that Lucifer is the younger brother of Jesus. Christians believe that Satan is a created being (Ezek. 28:12, 14–17).

• Mormons believe that everyone who has ever lived existed first as an "intelligence" who lived in eternal matter. The Bible teaches that every person had his or her beginning on earth at the time of conception (Ps. 139:13–16).

• The Mormon concept of salvation comes in two parts: general and individual. They believe that all humanity will be saved when they are resurrected and will be judged on their works. If a person wants to earn forgiveness from personal sins, he must meet certain requirements, including faith in Christ, baptism by immersion, obedience to the teachings of the Mormon Church, good works, and the keeping of the commandments of God. Christians believe that salvation is a free gift of God through faith not works (Rom. 6:23; 10:9; Eph. 2:8–9).

• Mormons believe that everyone must learn to become a god, the same as all gods have done, by moving from one small degree to another. The Bible is clear that there is only one God—none before and none after. He is changeless (Isa. 43:10; Hos. 11:9; Mal. 3:6).

• Mormons believe that the Trinity is three gods—with distinct bodies, except for the Holy Spirit, who has never been able to become a man and has only a spirit body. Christians believe that the Trinity is one God whose essence is found in three persons (John 1:3; Col. 1:16; 2 Cor. 5:19; Eph. 2:18; Gen. 1:26; Ps. 110:1; Isa. 7:14; 48:16; 61:1; 1 Cor. 8:6; Heb. 1:8–10; Acts 5:3–4; Deut. 6:4).

- Mormons accept as the "word of God" the *Book of Mormon, Doctrine and Covenants,* and *Pearl of Great Price;* they do not, however, accept the whole Bible because of errors in translation. They also believe that God continues to speak new revelations because they are necessary. Christians believe that there is no new revelation from God and that the Bible is complete and without error (2 Tim. 3:16; Jude 3; Gal. 1:8; 2 Pet. 1:3).

- Mormons teach that most of humanity will end up in one of three levels of heaven: telestial, terrestrial, or celestial. Eternal life in celestial heaven is only for Mormons. Christians believe that heaven is God's dwelling place (Ps. 73:25) and will be the home for all those who believe in the complete payment for personal sins accomplished by Jesus on the cross (1 John 4:10). Ultimately, heaven is to be in the presence of Christ (Luke 23:43; John 14:3; 2 Cor. 5:8; 1 John 3:2).

New Age Movement and Christianity

- New Agers believe that "all is one and one is all," that all of matter is interconnected. The Bible teaches something entirely different: "because by Him everything was created, in heaven and on earth, the visible and the invisible, whether thrones or dominions or rulers or authorities—all things have been created through Him and for Him. He is before all things, and by Him all things hold together" (Col. 1:16–17). God is separate from His creation. The Bible also tells us that we are separated from God because of our sin (Rom. 3:23). In New Age teaching there is no need for forgiveness because we are all one vast interconnected ocean.

- New Agers believe that "God is everything and everything is God." Christians believe that God is a person not an impersonal force. God is not an "it" or a "force." He is alive, and He is our personal Lord and Savior. The Bible is filled with His attributes, and they tell us what a great and awesome God He really is (Deut. 6:4; Eph. 1:3).

- New Agers believe that Jesus was nothing more than an enlightened master who came to understand that he was a "little god." Christians believe that Jesus was fully God and fully man. They believe that Jesus is the Creator and the Sustainer, who had no beginning and has no end (John 1:1; 8:57–58; 10:30; Titus 2:13; Heb. 2:16–18; Matt. 1:18; 4:2; Col. 2:9).

- New Agers believe that since we are all "little gods," we must become "cosmically conscious" of the fact that we are gods. Christians believe that we are not gods though we are created in God's image. He is the great and awesome God. The Bible teaches that we are to have no other gods before Him—including ourselves. Satan learned the hard way about trying to become his own god. That's the desire that got him kicked out of heaven in the first place (Gen. 1:26; Exod. 20:3; Ps. 77:3; Isa. 14:12–14).

- New Agers believe that there's no need for a savior because, as little gods, we can save ourselves. Christians believe we can't save ourselves, that salvation is a free gift from God. Jesus died on the cross to take the punishment for our sin so we could experience a new life and forgiveness for our sins. There is no second chance to come back and fix our mistakes. The Bible is clear when it says we die only once and then we are judged (Rom. 5:8; 6:23; Eph. 2:8–9; Heb. 9:27).

- New Agers believe the countries of the world are coming together. Christians believe that only God will create a new heaven and earth. There will not be harmony or peace in this world until Jesus—the Prince of Peace—comes to live in the hearts of people (Isa. 65:17; 9:6; 2 Thess. 3:16).

- New Agers believe that reality is determined by what we believe and truth is relative. Christians believe that God has placed the sense of good and evil in our hearts and that truth is absolute (John 8:32; 14:6; Rom. 2:15).

- New Agers believe that human nature is neither good nor bad but open to constant transformation. Christians believe that all of humanity is born in sin and each person is guilty before a holy God (Rom. 3:9–11, 23).

- New Agers believe we must get in touch with our inner child in order to develop a new way of thinking about old problems. Christians believe that we change the way we think by renewing our minds. We are capable of thinking only in human terms, but God enables us to have an eternal perspective as a result of being new creations in Christ. The way to fully develop this new way of thinking is to allow God to readjust our minds, and this only happens through the study and knowledge of His Word (Rom. 12:2; 2 Cor. 5:17).

- New Agers believe that revelation comes from a variety of sources. Christians believe that the Bible—God's inspired Word—is the only source of revelation (2 Tim. 3:16–17; Jude 3).

Wicca, Witchcraft, and Christianity

- Most Wiccans believe in some form of reincarnation. For witches, reincarnation is different from what a Buddhist or Hindu believes. Instead of endless "karma," witches view reincarnation as something positive that takes the soul upward in its advancement toward godhood. Christians do not believe there are additional chances to come back and keep advancing our soul to new levels. The Bible is quite clear when it says we die only once and then we are judged (Heb. 9:26–28; 2 Pet. 2:9).

- Wiccans believe they can influence reality through invoking invisible spirits and powers. They believe that magic is the craft of witchcraft. Using magic, witchcraft, or invisible spirits is detestable to God and something He will not tolerate (Deut. 18:9–13; Isa. 8:19).

- The Wiccan view of salvation can be summed up with this statement: "We can open new eyes and see that there is nothing to be saved from; no struggle of life against the universe, no God outside the world to be feared and obeyed." Christians believe that we are all born with a spiritual terminal disease called sin that causes us to disobey God and go our own willful way. This causes us to be separated from God. The remedy was Christ's death on the cross (Rom. 3:23; 6:23; Isa. 59:2; 1 Tim. 2:5; 1 Pet. 3:18).

- Wiccans believe that experience is a more important revelation than any code of belief, and it's more important to reveal your own truth than to rely on doctrine. Christians believe that the most important revelation of truth is the Bible (Ps. 119:47, 72, 97; 2 Tim. 3:16; Heb. 4:12).

- Wiccans worship the earth and creation. They recognize the divinity of nature and all living things. Christians believe in worshipping the Creator not the creation (Deut. 4:39; Rom. 1:25; Jude 25).

- Wiccans believe that people have their own divine nature: "Thou art Goddess, thou art God." Christians believe that even though we are created in God's image, humanity is still sinful and fallen (Gen. 1:26–27; Rom. 5:12). The Bible clearly teaches that all kinds of wickedness come from within a person not divinity (Jer. 17:9; Mark 7:14–23).

- Wiccans do not believe that Jesus was God in the flesh or creator of the universe. They view Jesus as "a great white witch who knew the Coven of Thirteen." The key principle that sets Christianity apart from any other religion is the belief that Jesus is God. One of the names for Jesus in the Bible is Immanuel— which means "God with us" (Matt. 1:21–23; John 1:1, 14, 18; 8:24; Phil. 2:5–6).

Jehovah's Witnesses and Christianity

- JWs believe that there is only one God; they do not believe in the Trinity. Christians believe that God is three totally coequal and eternal Persons who exist as one divine Being (Matt. 3:13–17; 2 Cor. 13:14).
- JWs believe that Jesus is God's Son and is inferior to Him. Christians believe that Jesus is divine, the second person of the Trinity (John 1:1; Col. 1:1–19; Phil. 2:5–11).
- JWs believe that Jesus was not raised bodily from the grave but as a spirit. Christians believe that Jesus did rise physically from the grave and showed Himself to many people (John 20:24–29; Luke 24:36–43).
- JWs believe that the earth will never be destroyed. Christians believe heaven and earth will "pass away" and that God will create new heavens and a new earth (Matt. 24:35; Isa. 65:17).
- JWs are taught to refrain from independent thinking and to strictly adhere to the decisions, guidance, and scriptural understanding of the Watchtower Society. Christians depend on guidance from the Holy Spirit as they study the Bible and learn to obey God not people (Acts 5:29; 17:11; 1 John 2:26–27).
- JWs believe that you can work for your salvation because of Christ's death. Christians believe that Jesus' death on the cross totally paid for all of humanity's sins and that salvation is a result of God's grace and is a free gift from Him (Rom. 3:24–25; 5:12–19; 1 Pet. 2:24).
- JWs believe that man does not have an immortal soul and that at death man's life force (spirit) leaves and no longer exists. Christians believe that man has an immortal and eternal soul (spirit) that at death goes to one of two places: to be with Jesus

or to wait for judgment (Luke 23:46; 2 Cor. 5:8; Phil. 1:22–23; John 5:24–30).

- JWs believe that Jesus invisibly returned to earth in 1914 and now rules from heaven. Christians believe that Jesus will return to earth physically and clearly (1 Thess. 4:1–17).

Satanism, the Occult, and Christianity

- Satanists believe that Satan is the prototype, the original pattern to be followed. Basically they accept Satan as a life principle concept worth following. Christians believe that Jesus is our example; He is the one we need to emulate. Jesus Himself said, "Follow me" (1 Cor. 11:1; Mark 8:34).

- Satanists believe they must acknowledge the power of magic as a way to obtain their desires. To deny the power of magic after having called upon it with success will result in the loss of all they have obtained. Christians believe that power is received from the Holy Spirit of God. God gives us the desires of our heart when we delight ourselves in Him (Acts 1:8; Ps. 37:4).

- Satanists call theirs the "unreligion" because it does not subscribe to the notion of a deity with human form or attributes, nor a being who must be worshipped. In other words, they have no personal God. Christians believe in a personal God who is self-existent, all-powerful, all-knowing, and who never changes (Job 42:1–6; Ps. 115:3; Mal. 3:6; Matt. 19:26).

- Occultists believe in practicing things like astrology, I Ching, palm reading, and scrying to answer questions about life and to predict the future. Christians believe that no one knows the future except God, and, therefore, we need to trust in Him. He has plans to give us hope and a future (Eccles. 8:7; Prov. 3:5–6; Isa. 41:23; Jer. 29:11).

- Occultists believe in using witchcraft, interpreting omens, telling the future based on signs, conjuring spells, and communicating with the dead. Christians believe that participating in any of these things is a sin and detestable in God's eyes (Deut. 18:10–12).

Appendix 3

Other Religions, Philosophies, and Spiritual Movements

Atheism. The denial of or lack of belief in the existence of God or gods. The term *atheism* comes from the Greek prefix *a-*, meaning "without," and the Greek word *theos,* meaning "deity."

Agnosticism. The view that we cannot know whether God exists or not.

Eckankar. A spiritual path, oftentimes called the "Religion of the Light and Sound of God."

Macumba. A religion that combines elements of Roman Catholicism and African native religions. It's similar to Vodun.

Postmodernism. Describes the philosophy of examining the nature of meaning and knowing although academics in many fields have debated over its precise definition. Postmodernists question the validity of the faith in science and rationalism that originated during the Enlightenment and became associated with the philosophy known as modernism. They also question whether anthropology is, or should be, a science.

Pluralism. Theory that reality is composed of many parts and that no single explanation or view of reality can account for all aspects of life. Pluralism also refers to the acceptance of many groups in society or many schools of thought in an intellectual or cultural discipline.

Rosicrucianism. An ancient religion dating back to the seventeenth century that combines elements of Egyptian Hermetism, Gnosticism, Jewish Cabalism, and other occult beliefs and practices.

Santeria. A mingling of African tribal religions and Catholicism, established by African slaves brought to the Americas and the Caribbean.

Tolerance. The capacity for recognizing and accepting religious or social characteristics that differ from one's own.

UFO cults. Groups who believe that extraterrestrial beings are attempting to communicate with us and lead humans to a higher plane of understanding.

Voodoo. An ancient religion combining ancestor worship, sorcery, charms, and spells. Those involved are extremely superstitious and use strange objects to worship.

Vodun. A Caribbean religion that combines Roman Catholicism and African beliefs.

Notes

Chapter One: Do All Religions Really Lead to God?

1. Michael Green, *But Don't All Religions Lead to God?* (Grand Rapids, Mich.: Baker Books, 2002), 24–25.

Chapter Two: What Does It Mean to Be a Christian?

1. Paul Enns, *The Moody Handbook of Theology* (Chicago, Ill.: Moody Press, 1989), 329.

Chapter Three: Islam

1. Wayne Parry, *Times and Transcript* newspaper (Moncton, New Brunswick), 13 January 2003, B 5.

2. Sura 96:1–5, quoted in Caesar E. Farah, *Islam* (Minneapolis, Minn.: Barron's Educational, 1994), 39.

3. Malise Ruthven, *Islam in the World* (New York: Oxford University Press, 1984), 128.

4. Brigadier S. K. Malik, *The Quranic Concept of War* (Dehli: Adam Publishers and Distributors, 1992), 1.

5. See Johannes J. B. Jansen, *The Neglected Duty: The Creed of Sadat's Assassins and Islamic Resurgence in the Middle East* (London: MacMillan, 1986).

Chapter Four: Buddhism

1. *Court Zen,* Online News Hour with Jim Lehrer, www.pbs.org/newshour, 16 June 2000.

2. Dean C. Halverson, ed., *The Compact Guide to World Religions* (Bloomington, Minn.: Bethany House Publishers, 1996), 59.

3. Ibid.

Chapter Five: Hinduism

1. Fritz Ridenour, *So What's the Difference?* (Ventura, Calif.: Regal, 2001), 95.

Chapter Six: Mormonism

1. Robert M. Bowman, "How Mormons Are Defending Mormon Doctrine," *Christian Research Journal* (Fall 1989), 26.

2. Ibid.

3. Walter Martin, *The Kingdom of the Cults* (Bloomington, Minn.: Bethany House Publishers, 1985), 181–82.

4. Fritz Ridenour, *So What's the Difference?* (Ventura, Calif.: Regal Books, 2001), 133.

5. "Excerpts from three addresses by Prophet Wilford Woodruff regarding the Manifesto," in *Doctrine and Covenants*, 292–93.

6. Joseph Smith, *Journal of Discourses* 6:3 (Liverpool: F. D. & S. W. Richards, 1851–85), and Joseph Fielding Smith, *Doctrines of Salvation* (Salt Lake City, Utah: Bookcraft, 1956), 1:10.

7. *Encyclopedia of Mormonism*, vol. 2, 379.

8. Ezra Taft Benson, *Teachings of the Prophet Ezra Taft Benson* (Salt Lake City, Utah: Bookcraft, 1988), 7.

9. *Journal of Discourses*, 6:4.

10. Orson Pratt, *Orson Pratt's Works* (Salt Lake City, Utah: Deseret News Press, 1945), 196, quoted in Marvin W. Cowan, *Mormon Claims Answered*, rev. ed. (Salt Lake City, Utah: Utah Christian Publications, 1989).

11. Martin, *The Kingdom of the Cults*, 180.

12. Ridenour, *So What's the Difference?* 135.

13. Martin, *The Kingdom of the Cults*, 183.

14. Joseph Smith, documented in *History of the Church* (Salt Lake City, Utah: Desert Book Co., 1978), 4:461.

15. *Encyclopedia of Mormonism*, vol. 1, 136.

16. Ridenour, *So What's the Difference?* 138.

Chapter Seven: The New Age Movement

1. *Time* magazine, 7 December 1987, 62.

2. Gallup News Service, Frank Newport and Maura Strausberg, "Americans' Belief in Psychic and Paranormal Phenomena Is Up over Last Decade," 8 June 2001.

3. Roy Rivenburg, "Golf with Deepak," *Los Angeles Times*, 3 May 2003, E-10.

4. George Barna, "Americans Most Likely to Base Truth on Feelings," 12 February 2002. Special report states only 22 percent of adults and 6 percent of teens believe moral truth is absolute.

Chapter Eight: Wicca and Witchcraft

1. Alan W. Gomes, "Truth and Error: Comparison Charts on Cults and Christianity," in *Zondervan Guide to Cults and Religious Movements*,

series ed. Alan W. Gomes (Grand Rapids, Mich.: Zondervan Publishing House, 1998), 68.

2. George A. Mather and Larry A. Nichols, *Dictionary of Cults, Sects, Religions and the Occult* (Grand Rapids, Mich.: Zondervan Publishing Company, 1993), 314–15.

3. Craig S. Hawkins, "Goddess Worship, Witchcraft and Neo-Paganism," in *Zondervan Guide to the Cults and Religious Movements*, 8–11.

4. Ibid., 10–11.

5. Fritz Ridenour, *So What's the Difference?* (Ventura, Calif.: Regal Books, 2001), 211.

6. Starhawk (Miriam Simos), *The Spiral Dance: A Rebirth of the Ancient Religions of the Great Goddess* (San Francisco, Calif.: Harper and Rowe, 1979), 84.

7. Ceisiwr Serith, *The Pagan Family: Handing the Old Ways Down* (St. Paul, Minn.: Llewellyn, 1994), 198.

8. Starhawk, *The Spiral Dance*, 13, 109.

9. Ibid., 14.

10. Prudence Jones and Caitlin Matthews, eds., *Voices from the Circle: The Heritage of Western Paganism* (Wellingborough, Northamptonshire, England, The Aquarian Press, 1990), 40.

11. Margot Adler, *Drawing Down the Moon: Witches, Druids, Goddess-Worshippers, and Other Pagans in America Today,* rev. and exp. ed. (Boston, Mass.: Beacon Press, 1986), 9.

12. Doreen Valienete, *An ABC of Witchcraft: Past and Present* (New York, St. Martin's Press, 1973), 14.

Chapter Nine: Jehovah's Witnesses

1. Richard Abanes, *Cults, New Religious Movements and Your Family* (Wheaton, Ill.: Crossway Books, 1998), 235–37.

2. Ron Carlson and Ed Decker, *Fast Facts on False Teachings* (Eugene, Ore.: Harvest House Publishers, 1994), 126.

3. *The Watchtower,* 1 May 1938, 169.

4. Ibid., 15 June 1957, 370.

5. Ibid., 1 March 1983, 25.

6. Ibid., 15 March 1969, 172.

7. Ibid., 1 May 1957, 274.

8. Ibid., 1 December 1981, 27.

9. Ibid., 1 May 1957, 274.

10. Ibid., 15 January 1983, 22.

11. Ibid., 27.

12. Ibid., 15 September 1911, 48.

13. Walter Martin, *Kingdom of the Cults* (Bloomington, Minn.: Bethany House Publishers, 1985), 120.

14. Robert H. Countess, *The Jehovah's Witnesses' New Testament* (Phillipsburg, N.J.: Presbyterian and Reformed Publishing Co., 1982), 91.

Chapter Ten: Satanism and the Occult

1. Anton LaVey, *The Satanic Bible* (New York: Avon Books, 1969).

2. Ibid.

3. Ibid.

4. George Barna, *Grow Your Church from the Outside In* (Ventura, Calif.: Regal Books, 2002), 73.

5. Ontario Consultants on Religious Tolerance, www.religious tolerance.org

Chapter Eleven: What Will You Do with Jesus?

1. Josh McDowell, *The New Evidence that Demands a Verdict* (Nashville, Tenn.: Thomas Nelson, 1999), 334.

2. Ibid., 334.

3. Ibid., 9.

4. Dean C. Halverson, *The Compact Guide to World Religions* (Bloomington, Minn.: Bethany House Publishers, 1996), 256.

5. Ibid., 12.

6. Josh McDowell, *Evidence That Demands a Verdict* (San Bernardino, Calif.: Here's Life Publishers, 1986), 127.

Contact Information

For more information or to purchase audio and videotape resources and other books by Steve Russo, as well as information on the *Real Answers* and *Life on the Edge Live!* radio programs, the *24/SEVEN* TV show, and citywide evangelistic campaigns or public school assemblies, please contact:

Real Answers with Steve Russo
P.O. Box 1549
Ontario, California 91762

(909) 466–7060
FAX (909) 466–7056

Email: Russoteam@realanswers.com

You can also visit our Web sites at
www.realanswers.com
or
www.steverusso.com

Also Available

The TruthQuest™ Inductive Student Bible (NLT)

Black bonded leather with
slide tab 1-55819-843-1
Paperback with Expedition
Bible Cover 1-55819-928-4
Expedition Bible Cover only
1-55819-929-2

Blue bonded leather with
slide tab 1-55819-849-0
Hardcover 1-55819-855-5
Paperback 1-55819-848-2

*The TruthQuest™ Share Jesus without Fear
New Testament* (HCSB) 1-58640-013-4

The TruthQuest™ Prayer Journal 0-8054-3777-0

The TruthQuest™ Devotional Journal 0-8054-3800-9

TruthQuest™ Books ————————————————

**Survival Guide:
The Quest Begins!**
by Steve Keels with Dan Vorm
0-8054-2485-7

Survival Guide Spanish Edition
**En Busca de la Verdad—
Plan de Accion**
0-8054-3045-8

**You Are Not Your Own:
Living Loud for God**
by Jason Perry of Plus One
with Steve Keels
0-8054-2591-8

**Am I the One?:
Clues to Becoming and Finding
a Person Worth Marrying**
by James R. Lucas
0-8054-2573-X

**Getting Deep: Understand What
You Believe about God and Why**
by Gregg R. Allison
0-8054-2554-3

**Living Loud:
Defending Your Faith**
by Norman Geisler & Joseph Holden
0-8054-2482-2

**Vision Moments:
Creating Lasting Truths in the
Lives of Your Students**
by Bo Boshers & Keith Cote
0-8054-2725-2

**Something from Nothing:
Understand What You Believe
about Creation and Why**
by Kurt Wise & Sheila Richardson
0-8054-2779-1

————————————————

Commentaries
Getting Deep in the Book of . . .
Luke: Up Close with Jesus
0-8054-2852-6
James: Christian to the Core
0-8054-2853-4
Romans: A Life and Death Experience
0-8054-2857-7
Revelation: Never Say Die
0-8054-2854-2
by Steve Keels & Lawrence
Kimbrough

Available at Your Local Book Retailer

BROADMAN
& HOLMAN
PUBLISHERS

www.broadmanholman.com/truthquest